'ol

dir

ιIVES FOR
S ι   LIBERATION

ugust 1,

~8.9ι

ωιrds .

Educational Alternatives for Colonized People

MODELS FOR LIBERATION

Educational Alternatives for Colonized People:

MODELS FOR LIBERATION

By
ROBERT L. WILLIAMS

Edited By
ANNE M. ST. PIERRE

DUNELLEN

NEW YORK • LONDON

Author's Note

This book is dedicated to my mother, Mrs. Alice J. Jones, my first grade teacher, and to my wife, Fannie Louise Williams, and to my children, Ron, Sandy, Angie and Gail.

It is also dedicated to those public school systems that have demonstrated strong commitments to providing quality education for all students. The school boards, the superintendents, the faculties and the communities of Berkeley, California, San Francisco, California, New Albany, Mississippi, and Minneapolis, Minnesota are to be commended for their efforts. The Minnesota State Department of Education is to be commended for guidelines and regulations relating to equal opportunities.

This book is finally dedicated to all colonized people and all others who share the goal of the colonized community: to prevail over those conditions that limit life styles and reduce life chances.

109761

International Standard Book Number 0-8424–0077-X
Library of Congress Catalogue Card Number 78-88214
Printed in the United States of America.

Table of Contents

Preface

The syndrome of racist retrenchment is nationally pervasive. We witness the emergence of conservative, anti-integrationist school boards and the election of law and order governors and mayors. While state legislators declare their commitments to equal opportunity for poor and minority groups, they hastily enact legislation opposing low income suburban housing.

We observe the conspicuous absence of enthusiasm to change the racist patterns of authority in Federal, state and local governmental institutions. Congress has yet to demand or devise a plan for school desegregation that is equally applicable to districts in the north, south, east and west, nor has the Supreme Court mandated such a plan or its implementation. There are still anti-integration amendments in Federal aid-to-education appropriations bills, and clauses in Federal guidelines that erect barriers to the desegregation of schools.

Local school boards, state boards of education and state legislatures appear to be as guilty as their Federal counterparts of acting on the ambiguous edge of political power, affirming the contention that educational excellence revolves on the wheel of politics.

If you are a member of a colonized American community, you have three choices when you attempt to provide a meaningful education for your child: You may continue to allow your child to participate in the all too often irrelevant, inadequate programs of many inner-city public schools; you may shirk your responsibility by enrolling your child in a private school, or you may work to improve the system—to force tax-supported schools to provide the educational requirements needed for educationally cheated colonized children to break the immoral self-perpetuating cycle of colonization.

Historically, changes in social or educational patterns have been made only in proportion to the purpose, persistence and power of the group demanding the change. Not only must colonized people realize that they are being systematically exploited but they must also be determined to put an end to the colonization through educational change.

Who are the colonized? If you are poor, you are colonized, if you are black, you are colonized. Any poverty-stricken black, Indian, Chicano, oriental or white American who is denied the options of better life styles and better life chances because of certain manifest forms of institutional and individual racism is colonized. Therefore, I am directing this book first to the colonized people and their children, and second to all those who share in the goal of liberation from the colony.

To colonized parents: This is literally a life and death struggle insofar as the education of your children is concerned because the colony has become a way of life for far too many people. You must have an unyielding conviction that there is a direct correlation between educational achievement and the survival of your children in a highly competitive technological society. This may be the last chance that colonized people will have to break through the barriers of the colony, not for this generation (they have already attended the schools of the colony) but for their children.

To educators: The time for high-toned useless rhetoric is past. The time is also past for the appointment of well-intentioned study committees to produce multitudes of smug, euphemistic recommendations which are rarely, if ever, implemented. It is now time to view colonized people not as mute acceptors of the inevitable, but as a politically potent concentration of voters who are dissatisfied with the present educational system and its retarding results on their children.

As a black American educator and as a black American parent, I share in the struggles of the colonized community to develop educational alternatives for their children—alternatives based on realistic goals as well as righteous indignation. I am not interested in a-rose-by-any-other-name models of education designed by the perpetrators of institutional colonization. Since these models refuse to admit to the presence of a colony, much less to an intrinsic perpetuation of the colony, I hold them to be invalid. The emphasis, therefore, will be on the creation of a model valid from a colonized perspective, the colonized perspective of one black educator.

Colonization was selected as a theme because it transcends the dimension of race. It is irrational to base the premise of colonization solely on white racism; colonization breeds black colonizers, and colonizes Whites as well. Colonizers come in two types, human (individual) colonizers and structural (institutional) colonizers, and will be discussed as they relate to alternatives for the present educational system. Colonization is a concept, a condition, and an attitude of those people caught in the bonds of colonization as well as for those doing the binding.

The concept of colonization has been discussed before in Kenneth Clark's *Dark Ghetto*, in Franz Fanon's *Wretched of the Earth* and in Hamilton's and Carmichael's *Black Power*. However, with the exception of the first chapter, I have used a minimum of quotation. No doubt I will have failed to satisfy the hunger of some critics for literary references to chew on and statistical tables to spit out. I have no apologies to offer them. This was not intended for publication in a learned journal, but as an aid to parents seeking a different kind of education for their children.

Finally, I acknowledge that some of my intellectual commitments and positions are somewhat contradictory. I do not condemn or repudiate the entire system of American public education. I propose alternatives to those aspects of the system which intrinsically deny a large portion of American society full access to the benefits of that system. Hopefully, the results of changes within the system will equip today's colonized children with the tools to successfully deal with that deliberately restrictive institution, that dehumanizing immoral social anachronism—the colony.

R.L.W.

Foreword

In a nation of increasing racial and ethnic polarization, Robert L. Williams, presently an Assistant Superintendent of the Minneapolis Public Schools, is a voice to be listened to with attentiveness and with commitment. His words are those of warning. His prescriptions are directed toward hope.

While addressed in style primarily to the black community, this book is for all educators and concerned citizens, both black and white. It is written in parts almost poetically. In other parts, its words move with the seeming coolness of a chemist. In this way, what Dr. Williams has to say combines a rare sensitivity with the hard-nosed good sense of a seasoned educator who happens, first of all, to express his deep sense of humanity as a black American.

Several themes, of crucial importance to every American, stand out in this significant contribution to our current educational debate. One is that black Americans—along with their red, tan, and Asiatic brothers and sisters—are the colonized and most deeply exploited people in America today. It follows that, whether consciously, unconsciously or both, white America is the colonizer. White America is, in this role, repressive and racist. Its institutions, its structures and its people are collectively the sometimes unwitting and mindlessly mechanistic operatives in the presently endemic processes of racism and repression which characterize, in a tragic way, so much of our nation's life.

To be mindful in a lively way of one's inheritance affords us with at least a launching pad from which to move toward more positive and promising patterns of behavior. For American education especially, this is the greatest importance. It is American education which confirms our colonist *status quo*. Yet education may work to create a new equilibrium or an equitable give-and-take which promises for Blacks and other colonized minorities liberation from being the victims of racism and repression. It may also promise, for white Americans, liberation from fulfilling their somewhat less than humane inherited roles as colonizers, as an unfortunate benefiters of prolonged exploitation and as primary perpetrators of the pro-white racism and repression which are endemic in the nation's life.

It is not the current mood of white America to prescribe positively for black fulfillment or for its own liberation from the fetters—and from the ill-gotten gain—which mark the wielders of one-sided power. Dr. Williams quotes Frederick Douglass in this regard, noting that it is always the oppressed who must strike the telling blow for freedom. Hence, the theme of black responsibility for re-humanizing American life runs throughout this challenging and important book. Whether one agrees or disagrees with any—or perhaps even with all—of Dr. Williams' thoughtful prescriptions is relatively unimportant. The basic significance of his book rests in its willingness to probe, to suggest, and to compel fresh responses to old and fruitless efforts which have served to entrap us all. It is Jean-Paul Sartre who, along with wise minds of many ages, raises for colonized peoples the world over the imperative duty which they alone may perform. It is the task of taking leadership, as their unique trust and responsibility, in reshaping the values and the life patterns of those whose minds have been enchained by the errant ways of exploitation, oppression and colonization of their fellow human beings.

Dr. Williams speaks of equity as an alternative to equality. In so doing, he echoes the words of Plato who cried out in his day against what he saw as a false equality which treats equally those who are "equal and unequal alike." Plato, like Aristotle, spoke of the need for equity as the highest form of justice in which unjust advantages are compensated for and where all are treated, not alike, but according to their due. Blacks in America serve their nation best in their advocacy of the "equity and restitution" which is an age-old principle in European and American law. It is consistent also with the Judeo-Christian ethic. Whatever falls short of equity, it must be seen, serves to short change us all. In the Sivahili Tongue, we speak of "Harembee," or the setting of all things right in ways which creation itself—and the best for all of mankind—decree. This is what we mean by equity.

In any probing discussion of American education, the question of relative I.Q.'s or of Intelligence Quotients is certain to be raised. Dr. Williams meets the issue head on. He sees the the current contrasts between black and white intelligence as being without foundation. What our standard tests measure, he notes, is the capacity to survive and to succeed in a middle-class dominated and colonialist-minded society. We might, on this basis, simply call such tests "Survival Quotient" (S.Q.) tests rather than Intelligence Quotient Tests. What Dr. Williams might have added, as implicit in such line of thought, is that genius—or essential intelligence—is most clearly evidenced among those who suffer. Genius is the capacity to empathize, that is, to enter by the imagination into the inner life or workings of a person, of a process or of an epoch in the lives of others. The alienated in every household tend naturally to be empathizers. So also with the alienated or oppressed in any society. In this sense, black Americans and other colonialized minorities may possess proportionately more of the makings of true intelligence or of genius, at this juncture in our common life, than their fellow white Americans. Of most immediate importance are, first, the need to differentiate between intelligence and survival skills and, second, to devise ways to measure the genius-related intelligence of which we speak.

A new mood of self-awareness and of self-acceptance is abroad in the black community. It began in the mid-1960's when the shoe of institutionalized white racism at last, pinched black Americans for harder than they could bear. It was then that the black segment of America saw the need to understand life in a vastly new and more realistic light and then to "tell it like it is." Our beloved Chicano and Indian brothers and sisters, of late, have joined vocally and dramatically in this same experience.

For those who renounce oppression and call us to new and more rewarding ways of action we must be especially grateful. For this reason, we must receive the alarming insights of those who cry out in anger and displeasure at the oppression and exploitation which have now come to be an established part of our American way of life. It is on behalf of such Americans who would summon us from what may be a sleep of death to a fresh awakening that our brother, in this volume, speaks. Hear him. Heed his words. Improve, or build wherever we can, upon what he has to say. We turn away listlessly only to our peril.

Nathan Wright, Jr.
Professor of Urban Affairs
State University of New York at Albany

CHAPTER ONE

The Central City Colony

"A colony is a community of segregated/isolated people whose life-styles and life-chances are dictated by economic and political influences outside the colony."

R. L. WILLIAMS

Every major city in America harbors a colony. Concentrated by housing patterns, isolated by freeway systems, castrated by the socio-economic structure, inhabitants of the central city are as effectively colonized as any 19th century British outpost. But 20th century colonization is far more malicious than the territorial imperialism of the British; this is a colonization of Americans by other Americans. This colonization is also motivated by the desire for economic and political power, but the justification for continuing social control is the conviction that white control is better than black control . . . that the white mind is more intelligent than the black mind . . . that white skin is better than black skin . . . in short, the conviction of racism.

1

Just as the central city is polluted, the air by factory smoke and automobile exhausts, the water by industrial and human wastes, the land by industrial, governmental, and financial complexes and by crowded housing patterns, so too is society polluted—the minds of the people are polluted by the poison of racism. Racism is perpetrated and perpetuated throughout the economic, political, educational, social and religious institutions of America. Racism is a pollution; racism hides behind a smoke screen of reasonable attitudes; racism is a waste because it wastes human potential. Institutional racism arises from legitimized social arrangements within and between social institutions. It then follows that the real polluters are those individuals behind the institutions that maintain and extend racism.

The central city colony is inhabited by people who are forced into limited life styles and life chances because of certain manifest forms of individual and institutional racism. Its population is socially controlled by economic and political power structures outside of the colony. The colonizers are the policy makers within the structures whose decisions and actions determine the roles of others. The ghetto school is the perpetuating agent of the colonizers, teaching children behavior and attitudes that will insure the existence of the colony in its present form.

Balance of power is more than a political philosophy for the colonizers. It is a necessity if they are to maintain their roles in the superimposed economic and political structures they have so painstakingly created. Colonizers must preserve the existing distribution of power if they are to maintain the tenuous equilibrium of a colonized society. Power means control.

The first step in establishing a colony is to concentrate the population. It takes less effort and power to manipulate a physically consolidated mass than a fragmented, dispersed band of individuals. It is no accident that in most cities the freeway system just happens to divide low-income and minority districts—the ghettoes—from the rest of the city. The freeway

system is one of the physical means used to maintain a disproportionate balance of power by isolating a certain population
from the rest of the city's inhabitants and, consequently, from
the sources of economic, political and social power.

The freeway is inconsistent with the economic principle
which stresses that certain economic advantages can be had
through the consolidation of fragmented entities into one
concentrated structure. Although it is true that freeways
bring commuters into the city, the same freeways bring the
same commuters back to their homes in the suburbs. Freeways often divert the flow of traffic away from stores and
businesses in the colony to shopping centers in the suburbs
or to the heart of the business district—neither of which
contribute significant revenue to the running of the city
proper. The freeway is a direct contributor to the loss of
central city revenue. This has immediate consequences for
the city government and the education of colonized children,
for while the tax base is being reduced, there is an increase
in cost to provide needed educational and social services.

However, freeway designers think nothing of routing a
freeway through low-income residential areas of the central
city. Rarely does a right-of-way disturb homes in more affluent neighborhoods. The routing of freeways through ghetto
residential areas serves only to further concentrate and
isolate the colony, for the residents of the homes that stood
where the freeway now stands have nowhere to go but can
only retreat further into the colony. They cannot afford homes
or apartments in the fringes and suburbs outside the central
city, nor are they welcome in them. They have no choice but
to move deeper into the already overpopulated ghetto, crowd-
ing into existing housing (for there is no more land to build
new houses) or move to a different city, where conditions are
the same as those they left. The inhabitants of the colony
can get almost anywhere on the freeway system—anywhere
except out of the ghetto.

The concentrating effect of a freeway on housing patterns
is the same for poor Whites, poor Blacks, poor Indians or just

poor. But more specifically, the freeway is a major contributor to racial concentration and isolation, especially between city and suburbs. The National Advisory Commission on Civil Disorders has warned that American society is polarizing into two societies: separate and unequal, Black and White. The Commission cites statistics on the disparity of the racial distribution between the city and the suburbs. The Commission contends that racial/economic polarization is advancing at an astronomical rate, and threatens to petrify racial isolation into perpetuity. (Speaking of transportation systems, it is ironic that those who oppose busing programs to achieve school desegration fail to recognize the wheel as the great paradox of our time. It was the wheel that aided the flight to the suburbs, the wheel that necessitated the freeway systems, so the wheel should be the tool to reverse the pattern of racial imbalance in the schools.)

The second step in creating a colony is to establish the base of power outside the perimeters of the colony. The colonized population must not have access to the power base or the means to achieve or create a rival power structure. The pollution of racism and the phenomenon of power are cyclic. The colonizer, from his vantage point outside the colony, manages a self-perpetuating economic/political machine. White middle- and upper-class Americans are heirs to an economic heritage based on the control and exploitation of certain segments of the population: the poor, the minorities, the uneducated.

To retain the power base, the colonizer must defend and maintain the current system. He also must not let the uninitiated have real control (power) over any situation; he cannot share power or let the colonized reach a point where they can challenge how existing power is used. Fear of loss of power is a prime cause of racism. The colonizer must keep the people under his control, "Subject peoples, victims of the greed, cruelty, insensitivity, guilt, and fear of their masters." (Kenneth Clark, *Dark Ghetto*, Harper and Row, 1965, p. 11.) Therefore, the colonizer will use already existing social institutions to keep the powerless from even seeking power. It is not accidental that there are twice as many unemployed black adults as there are white adults. It is not coincidental that the nation's largest banks are controlled by Whites and hold more than half of the nation's total assets, and that the parceling out of these monies in business and home loans is done by Whites. Nor is it a coincidence that investment of these bank funds is in companies and corporations controlled by Whites. The same pattern is followed in the educational system: the school buildings enrolling the highest number of poor and minority students are invariably the oldest; educational programs are frequently substandard; instructional material and equipment is scarce and outdated; students are shunted into vocational programs instead of college prep courses; achievement scores are the lowest in the city; but most of all, the schools do not now offer the means that would give colonized people access to power. The colony and the existing system are indelibly stamped on them as a way of life from which there is no escape. The propaganda of the colonizer is taught with all the fervor of the sacred word.

The means which the colonized must now acquire to live in their present situation is a repertoire of survival skills. This must include cognitive internalization of the many unwritten rules and tactics of the economic and politcal systems around which the colonizer wields his position of power. But different kinds of means are needed if the colonized are to achieve access to power.

The means to achieve a stabilized colonized community is a manpower pool of skilled and semi-skilled people who can contribute to the economic, political and educational liberation of the colony. The means to the acquisition of marketable skills and development of economic power bases in the colonized community is education. The means for children of the colonized are educational skills including basic literacy, communications, and computational skills.

Means for the colonized people, individually and collectively, is land. A people without land, without territory, are a people without dignity or direction. Without direction, a people can have no destiny.

History has documented man's incessant quest for territory. Ardrey writing in *African Genesis* and the *Territorial Imperative* details early man's basic drive for the acquisition, maintenance and expansion of territory and use of the land as a power base. Land was a major factor n the Russian revolution, the French revolution, and the American revolution. The quest for land was a major factor in the expansion of both the British and American empires. Countries did not conquer lands just because territory is a nice thing to have. Control of the land meant control of the economic system—or—power.

A recent visit to Mississippi has led me to the conclusion that there is a definite connection between human dignity and land ownership, and that black reconstruction in the South is an affirmation of that dignity. In today's South there are black-owned businesses, not black-fronted (white-owned/black-managed) as is frequently the case in the North. There are more black tradesmen earning a good living in the South than in the North. It is not uncommon to see black brickmasons working in the South—a rare phenomenon in the North. Blacks in the South are aggregating economic and political power to an extent unparalleled in the North. School desegregation in the South has eclipsed that in the North and West. A Russian Czar criticized Lincoln for freeing the slaves without providing them with land and tools so they could begin their freedom with dignity. Although colonization and slavery officially ended in 1863 with the Emancipation Proclamation, we find rampant colonization in the welfare and credit system. Same song, different verse: the roles remain fundamentally unaltered—the land owning colonizer and the landless colonized. What dignity can be found in a rat-infested, overcrowded slum? What is motivating about a highrise catacomb where living yet mentally dead zombies wander aimlessly, seeking escape from a life of joblessness, hopelessness, and heroin.

The individual's need for territory, psychological as well as physical, can be a strong motivating force for human behavior.

Land ownership is basic to the struggle of colonized people, just as the unwillingness to share territory is basic to the colonizer. In the economic system, territoriality emerges in the struggle between large corporations and small businesses. In education, there is a territorial struggle for power between faculties and school administrations, between the students and their teachers, between rival professional groups, and between the school administration and the community.

There is inevitable conflict in the colony when the same means is used to obtain opposite goals. This is particularly true when the goals of the colonizer and the colonized are perceived by each to be mutually exclusive. Goals derive from needs that are often translated into perceptions of role and role expectation.*

Goals then determine what roles an individual must assume to achieve them. The roles that an individual assumes are directly related to what he perceives as valid means to a goal. There are even greater chances for conflict when not only are the goals of the colonizer and the colonized at cross purposes, but when both groups seek unrealistic goals. But what is realistic and what is not? What is realistic for the colonizer might well be quite unrealistic for the colonized.

Realistic goals are those that are clearly perceived and within the grasp and ultimate attainment of the individual. It would be unrealistic for colonized people to expect that power

---

*The psychologist Heider has described goals as external phenomena seen as useful to the restoration and maintenance of the individual's equilibrium. This is consistent with the theory of optimization and the homeostatic principle which states that man chooses from the alternatives available to him those he sees as restoring equilibrium. The homeostatic principle assumes that man is in a constant state of equilibrium because of intrinsic phenomena that Maslow has identified as needs. Refining Maslow and Heider, it is possible to say that the individual has a continuing need to achieve a state of equilibrium, a balance between his nomothetic dimension (the individual's relation to the norms of society) and his idiographic dimension (the individual's personal needs). Thus a perceived goal promises the individual restoration to equilibrium; if he is successful in achieving the goal, he is, behaviorally speaking, reinforced.

will ever be willingly shared by their colonizers. It would be unrealistic for colonized parents to expect that the colonized school will ever receive an equitable proportion of per-pupil expenditures, although there will continue to be strong rhetoric from the colonizer proclaiming his commitment to the goals of *equal educational opportunity*—beautiful words, but with a hollow ring.

Equal educational opportunity, in the first place is impossible in a society in which power is unequally distributed. Secondly, the presentation of an opportunity does not make allowance for the readiness of the individual to take advantage of that opportunity. Thus, the concept of equal education opportunity is analagous to a footrace between a finely honed athlete and an overweight, out-of-shape businessman. Both, it is true, are starting from the same point, both are beginning the race at the same time, but are they really getting equal starts? And so for equal education opportunity to ever be a reality and a realistic goal for colonized children, there must first be what Nathan Wright calls a *relative proportionate compensatory closing of the gap* between the unfairly advantaged colonized brother. This would mean, in industry, preferential consideration for colonized persons in hiring and promotions. In the educational system, it would mean direct promotions of minority group persons until they are proportionally represented at every level of school administration, from custodian to superintendent. Certainly there will be charges of preferential treatment and "racism in reverse" from those who oppose the concept of compensatory closing of the gap . . . those who, in essence, advocate maintaining the status quo, the colonizer/colonized relationship.

A desirable alternative to equal educational opportunity is *Equity of Program Option*. Under the equity of program option concept every program course offering in a public school system would be equally available to every pupil in that school system as his option, according to his ability and his needs. Equity of program option implies an equity in per-pupil allocations within a school district, between districts within a state, and ultimately, equity in per-pupil allocations among states. This further implies the responsibility of the Federal government in insuring every American child access to educational programs that are commensurate with his ability and needs.

Hence, given the inequities within the colony as it exists today, a more realistic educational goal for colonized people would be an educational system based on equity of program option, not on the fantasy of equal educational opportunity.

Goals can become unobtainable when the premises underlying the individual's perception of the goal are distorted. In education, one such goal dilemma caused by distorted premises is the long-standing theory that the smaller the class, the better the teaching and learning results. This premise is predicated on the false assumption that teaching, and learning process, is something that teachers do *to* children. A careful analysis discloses that this is really a sublimation of the learning process to the teaching process—a sublimation of the child (and his educational needs) to the teacher. This view will orient classroom methods around teacher-centered activities rather than learner-centered activities. If, on the other hand, the teacher is oriented to what the learner must accomplish to fill his (the learner's) particular needs, then, in many instances, it may turn out that large classes could be best for that particular child.

A critical goal for colonized parents is the educational achievement of their children. Essential to the attainment of this goal is the mastery of basic communication and computation skills at the same level as those with whom they will be in competition—the children of the colonizer. Any minimizing of this goal for colonized children is a failure to recognize the colonizer's goal—the maintenance and expansion of the colony through science and technology. Of necessity, there is little place in the society for those who cannot communicate and compute in the language of that society.

The humanists will argue that educational offerings should be geared toward a classical, liberal arts type of preparation. They say that man is the maker of society, and therefore, to function in a society you must know about man and all his accomplishments. I do not disagree with their theory; but the colonized community simply does not have the time for this. The reality for colonized people is now: not tomorrow, not yesterday. Technology and science are here *now*. They are where the power is. The colonized child, already without power, and the means to power, from birth, will be unable to compete in a technological society with a humanistically oriented education. The increasing unemployment rates for unskilled workers should be a sobering reminder to colonized parents that school is where their children's life-styles and life-chances will be shaped.

But goals, nevertheless, are central to colonizer/colonized role relationships. In power negotiations between the colonizer and the colonized, both parties focus on the perceived attractiveness of the goal and the probability of achieving it. The potential for conflict increases when the goals become unrealistic, or when either party overestimates or underestimates the attractiveness of the other's goal. For instance, the case of the Vietnam war, the Johnson administration perceived a goal different from that of the American public, pursued that goal to an unreasonable length, and disastrously underestimated the attractiveness of their goal (ending the war) to the voting public.

Individual perceptions of a common goal are fundamental to the development of a strong and united community power base from which to enter into negotiations with the colonizer. (The operating psychological premise is the theory of optimization, which states that the individual chooses from the alternatives available to him those he perceives as having optimum utility for reaching his goals.) The colonizer will be interested in negotiating only when he perceives that the colonized possess some means to upset the equilibrium of the colony.

The colonized can only negotiate from an existing power base because the colonizer will not recognize or admit to *potential* power. The colonized must also be able to recognize the effectiveness of the power base. There are five prerequisites for

the formation of an effective power base:
1) The colonized must have a service or product needed (service or product can be read as anything the colonized people have that the colonizer wants, such as a bloc of votes) or desired by the colonizer.
2) The service or the product must be critical to maintaining the equilibrium of the colony—especially to the economic system.
3) The value of the service or product must exceed in quality or desirability any alternative the colonizer can offer. The colonized community has made the mistake of sharing its secrets and inventions too soon. Oftentimes the actual inventor or discoverer of a process receives no substantial reward for his contribution because he does not have the means to develop it. All contemporary folk and jazz music is based on the rhythm and blues of the black community, yet the enormous profits from the recording industry go to the large corporations that had the resources to exploit the discovery of folk and jazz music.
4) The colonized must be aware of the worth of the product or service and its importance to the colonizer. The colonized community must be aware of its power.
5) The colonized community must be united enough to exert pressure on the colonizer when necessary.

In power negotiations, a functional approach to positive reconciliation is necessary to change the balance of power. The "I have something that you want, and I know you want it, so what will you give me for it" approach is an attitude that the colonizer recognizes and even admires. It is one that he has used repeatedly with evident success. The colonized community can benefit from the examples of the pressure tactics used by activist student groups, powerful suburban taxpayer associations, legislative lobby groups such as the oil and labor union groups, and the increasing racial/ethnic militant organizations. These groups engage in tactics to strengthen their position in negotiations with the colonizer. Understanding and use of successful pressure tactics are skills needed by the colonized community for effective negotiation with the colonizer.

The concepts of role and perception are, in the real world, inseparable. Sociologists refer to roles as alter-reference assigned expectancies. The individual assigns himself roles by his own perceptions, by his own actions, and in response to actions of others. Role position is critical to and influenced by what a person perceives. Conversely, what a person perceives may be traced to expected behavioral consequences assigned to a certain role position. For example, the judgment of an individual as to what constitutes "law and order" and the expected behavior he assigns to the role of a "law-abiding citizen" are based on perceptions of his own and other people's reaction to what he understands as law and order. Actions and reactions are based on what a person sees, understands, or perceives, or what he *thinks* he sees.* From the position of what he perceives law and order to be, and the behavior he expects because of that perception, the colonizer will condemn the looting and burning of urban areas, ascribing the blame to shiftless minority groups, particularly the Blacks. Blacks are seen as breaking what the colonizer perceives as the law, and therefore should be punished according to the letter of the law. But what about the Black's concept of law and order? An analysis of the "unlawful" behavior of the colonizer brings to focus crimes of equal, if not greater, magnitude than those ascribed to shiftless minorities. It is legal for national political figures to be beneficiaries of tax write-offs. It is all right that lobby-induced legislation gives a bonus of some thirty-seven billion dollars to the oil industry under the guise of a depletion

---

*Remember the optical illusion of the goblet and the cameo? What appears to be the image of a white goblet is centered on a black background. The eye is drawn to the white part of the picture and we see a goblet. By focusing on the black portion to the sides of the pictures, the profile of two cameos facing each other immediately becomes evident. Your reaction to the picture, and your resulting behavior, depends on what you perceive when you look at the picture —the goblet or the faces.

allowance. It has been established by Congressional investigations that the present income tax system favors big business and wealthy individuals; there arc enough loop-holes and tax-dodges so very wealthy individuals can pay very little, if any, personal tax. It is illegal for protesting students to block traffic, but quite legal for suburban governments to blockade the inner-city with restrictive housing codes, zoning laws, and state-supported legislation against low-income housing. It is all right that freeway systems can cut through inner-city residential areas but never disturb wealthy suburban neighborhoods. It has been documented that rural and urban Americans are going hungry while large farmers are paid to plow fields under, and thousands of tons of grain are in storage to keep up the price of grain. While millions of people are crowded into highrise slums, corporations gulp acres of land forfeited for tax payments. How is this possible? Because the colonizer's political system supports the colonizer's economic system, and all are under the sanction of the law. That is power.

The black American has been looted of his most precious possession—his heritage. Taken as human cargo aboard slave ships to an alien land, he was robbed of his dignity, and stripped of the possession that Western civilization calls the cornerstone of society—the family unit. Looted as his cultural identification, he was given a label connoting a role of sub-servience—negro—until recently, spelled with a small "n" to signal the colonizer's definition of the role relationship between American Whites and American Blacks. Looting and burning can take place in education when, because of inequities in the property tax system, affluent suburban school districts have a greater per pupil expenditure than their inner city counterparts. Looting and burning can be the crippling pre- and post-natal environment that deprives a fetus of proper nourishment needed by the developing cells; it can be an environment that deprives a fetus of proper nourishment needed by the developing cells; it can be an environment that deprives the newborn of stimulants needed for physical and mental development.

Colonized people have a far different perception of law and order, and who is to say whose is the most valid? The colonized people, through hard and bitter experience, have come to recognize a dichotomy in law and order. What they see is law for the colonizers and order for the colonized. They have come to view the concepts of justice and due process of law as empty phrases, something to hide behind, no different from the sheets of the Klan. The colonized have been promised justice and legal equality. What he has been given are riots, jail sentences and killings when he has dared to assert his rights as an American citizen. He has heard civil rights programs voiced by Presidents (voiced, but not supported) and he has seen the leaders of the movements become martyrs to their convictions. For the colonizer, law is a shield behind which to build and defend an economic empire that in turn becomes his protection from the law.

The philosophical basis for all law is a symbolic representation of a moral judgment. Morality implies absolutism with its underlying assumption that truth is absolute. Ethics, on the other hand, begins with man and acknowledges his human strengths and weaknesses. Moral law demands that there be some deciding authority. Who is the deciding authority? He who has the power. In the colony, it is the colonizer. Moral law becomes an imposition of a normative behavior according to a predetermined set of absolutes and is, in reality, not law but coercion.

Before the colonized can ever perceive of law and order as having any meaning for their community, the application of justice in the ethical as well as the legal sense must be made more equitable. The mechanism is already there, the Fourteenth Amendment to the Constitution of the United States prohibits any state from denying to any person equal protection under the law. We must go one step further in assuring them protection before the colonized are looted of their most valuable possession— the intellectual development of their children. States are prohibited from denying equal protection of the law; they must now be made to fulfill their obligations to educate all children on an equal basis. The inequities between educational offerings in suburban school districts and central city systems has been discussed, but it is worth discussing again. The California Supreme Court has ruled that the property tax system used to finance education in California could be ruled unconstitutional because districts with low tax bases could not educate children on an equal basis with affluent districts having broad tax bases and high property valuation. Most states use property tax formulas similar to California's; court cases have been instituted in many of them. Eventually the question will reach the U.S. Supreme Court. At that time the colonized community will see whose perception of law and order is most valid—theirs or the colonizer's.

Perception of roles is also a cause for conflict in power negotiations between the colonizer and the colonized. As the colonized community gains power, roles will be altered. When the colonized individual refuses to accept his "assigned" role and assumes a new one that he has defined himself, he also changes the role of the colonizer. (This causes hostility and conflict since established perceptions and roles, even those that are unrealistic, are not easily abandoned.) By refusing to accept a role subordinate to that of the colonizer, he will modify his behavior accordingly so that he ceases, even refuses, to see himself as colonized. He discovers in the process of power negotiations what behavioral scientists have known for a long time—that *both* the colonizer and the colonized must play roles to sustain the equilibrium of the colony.

In the process of altering the balance of power, the economic and political pretexts for the maintenance of the colony are stripped away and the underlying yet overriding conviction of racism is revealed as self-evident. The colonizer's assurance of his role is based on his perception of the established concepts of "the way it's supposed to be." It is a traumatic experience for most people to admit that their perception of reality was false and that their roles must be changed to fit new perceptions. Most people will admit that racism is intrinsically

wrong; what they will not admit is that they are racists.*
The colonizer will use every method available to him to evade
admitting that he is a colonizer and that his empire is racist-
oriented, for if his perceptions of the system change, then his
role must change accordingly. Power has never been willingly
shared.

A typical colonizer tactic to evade facing up to the issue of
racism is to shield himself behind what I have come to view as
a self-protective barrier. One example illustrating the dynamics
of the self-protective barrier is the open community meeting
where school desegregation, and more specifically, busing
will be discussed.

Generally, there are three distinct groups in the audience:
the pro-integrationists, the anti-integrationists, and the middle-
of-the-roaders. The largest and most vocal group are the anti-
integration forces. They have been alerted by a bulletin in
their mailboxes, sometimes distributed by a panicky school
principal, but usually some anti-integrationist group. The
bulletin announcing a hearing on busing is worded to play on
the fears, emotions, and prejudices of parents. There is a sketch
of a bus under a boldface headline, "**DO YOU WANT YOUR
CHILD BUSED ACROSS TOWN?? ATTEND THE BUS-
ING HEARING IN THE SCHOOL GYM TONIGHT AT
7:30!! HELP KEEP OUR CHILDREN IN OUR NEIGHBOR-
HOOD.**" The stage is now set for a showdown between groups
that will never get around to discussing educational programs

---

*It is pathetic to hear white parents attempt to justify their actions in
taking their children out of "paired" or "clustered" schools where
busing is required to achieve racial balance. They contend they are
not against pairing per se, but don't wish their children taken out
of the neighborhood or fatigued by long bus rides. These same
parents will send their children to all white private schools in the
suburbs, where not only are the children taken out of the neighborhood, but the bus ride to the all white private school is up to three
and four times as long as to the paired school. These parents are
hiding behind their children, manufacturing excuses, because they
refuse to admit that they do not want their children to sit next to a
child of a different color.

for children. Any chance for rational discussion has been negated by the bulletin.

The gymnasium is filled to capacity by 7:00 p.m. The meeting is chaired by a community person who makes the point early in the evening that his private views on busing are irrelevant since he is acting only as moderator. On stage, facing the audience, is a panel of community people and school district central administration personnel. The school board has ordered the meeting to determine some kind of community consensus before making its official position known. The open meeting becomes a temperature check of the community. More than likely, one of the district administrators is black—a visible representative of the colonized community. The presence of a black person assumes the causal variable in the social problem is black, and therefore the solution to the problem of racial imbalance is the burden of the Black. Because of his visibility, the black administrator becomes heir to a racist-oriented role based more on his color than his expertise. The subtle form of racism is openly manifest at the open meeting where the black panelist receives a disproportionate share of the questions, insults and enmity directed at him from the audience. The height of the insult to the black panelist are the tongue-in-cheek acknowledgements from the audience that he is suddenly some "authority" on that colonizer-created malady—the pollution of racism. There is a conspicuous absence in the audience of the Blacks whose children are presumed by anti-integrationists to be the recipients of desegregation—another racist presumption.

The dynamics of the self-protective vacuum unfolds as the meeting progresses. There are five major components of the self-protective vacuum. First, there is the *Race and Emotional Blindness Barrier*. Behind this barrier, the anti-integrationist evades the issue of racism simply by ignoring any facts supporting integration. He is likely to argue, for example, that when one speaks of poverty, he is speaking of Blacks or other minorities. He ignores the statistics showing that most persons living in poverty in America are white. He is prone to argue that the Federal government is spending too much money on shiftless Blacks, that too much of his tax dollars goes to subsidize welfare programs for Blacks. Again, he will ignore the fact that nearly half of the total national budget goes for military spending, less than one-fourth for health, education and welfare programs. He will close his mind to labor statistics delineating the economic disparities between Blacks and Whites with the argument that Blacks have the same opportunities as Whites.

Secondly, there is the *Barrier of Open Defiance Of the Law.* From this position, the anti-integrationist will argue the morality of law and order, yet at the same time he will openly proclaim his defiance by opposing the right of elected school boards to exercise their authority to regulate schools within their jurisdictions . . . and that includes the authority of a local school board to take the necessary steps to correct racial isolation within its schools. The anti-integrationist will argue vehemently against mandatory busing because it is the use of force he opposes. The madness of his logic leads him to perceive the daily transportation of students on educational excursions to museums, zoos, and other related transportation involved activities as "not really busing, but more of a field trip". Further, he complains about the excessive costs of busing involved in the pairing of two nearby schools in favor of a citywide voluntary cluster program in which schools have specialized programs that may be shared on an "integration" basis, once or twice a month . . . which incidentally, involves triple the transportation costs of pairing schools. He is against the school board using its legal authority in assigning children to school buildings, yet he has little difficulty accepting the force of government behind traffic laws, income taxes, and mandatory military service. He is quick to point out a glaring ambiguity by asserting that segregation is prohibited by the Constitution although it does not require integration . . . a great play on words.

Thirdly, there is the *Last Ditch Stand Barrier.* Behind this barrier, the anti-integrationist will resort to irrational and emotionally laden pronouncements as, "We need documented scientific evidence that integration works, that it will provide better quality educations for our children." His definition of quality education is predicted on segregated, isolated neighborhood schools. Further, he will ignore the fact that the scientific premises upon which our society rest derive from the phenomenon called intuitive reason. Who can prove that fatherhood is better than motherhood, that love is better than hate? Certainly these are not provable by scientific criteria, yet it does not stop us from making judgments and decisions. In the face of losing support, the anti-integrationist will resort to the ultimate emotional appeal . . . "would you want your daughter to . . ."

Fourthly, there is the *Recognition of Facts and Inconsistencies Barrier*. Once the anti-integrationist begins to recognize the inconsistencies in his own thinking, the logical weaknesses in his own arguments, he is likely to begin his search for other alternatives . . . either to support his position, or to disprove the position of his challengers, the panel and pro-integrationists.

Fifthly, there is the *Recognition of New Roles Barriers*. Once the anti-integrationist has come to face the inconsistencies in his own thinking and has internalized some sense of ethical concern, the process of role re-examination begins. If he has had the fortune during the course of his discussion that evening to surmount the five barriers, he will begin to acknowledge, if not agree to, the need for new role relationships. He will arrive at a state of readiness to begin to liberate himself from the self-protective vacuum. He will advance toward meaningful communication with human beings he has heretofore thought of as invisible people.

When the colonizer admits to false perceptions, roles, and goals, and makes positive steps to alter his behavior and establish communication, the colonized community must be prepared to alter its behavior pattern and tactics. Growth is relative to power, and power can only be measured against other power. Earlier in this chapter, I outlined the steps necessary to achieve a power base from which to negotiate. I strongly advocated a united front against the colonizer, a solidarity amounting to self-imposed racial isolation. The colonized community must go through a period of transitory separatism; it must, as Carmichael and Hamilton argue in *Black Power,* close ranks. This is not a new concept, nor is it un-American. America has historically been a pluralistic society composed of multiple racial and ethnic solidarities. But once the colonized community has achieved an equitable share of the power necessary to be included in any decision-making process, it must renounce its self-imposed isolation. Once the community has established the necessary economic, political, and educational power bases necessary to insure not merely survival, but aggrandizement, it must move out into the larger circle of society:

> No nation can now shut itself up from the surrounding world and trot around the same old path of its fathers without interference. The time was when such could be done . . . Knowledge was then confined and enjoyed by the privileged few, and the multitude walked on in mental darkness. But a change has come over the affairs of mankind. Walled cities and empires have become unfashionable. The arm of commerce has borne away the gates of the strong city. Intelligence is penetrating the darkest corners of the globe . . . Oceans no longer divide, but link nations together, thoughts expressed on one side of the Atlantic are distinctly heard on the other . . . Africa must rise and put on her unwoven garment. Ethiopia shall stretch out her hand . . .
> *Frederick Douglas (Great Lives Observed),*
> © 1968, Prentice-Hall, Inc.

And so, for the American community, it is imperative that there be a change in affairs for the colonized, for the colonizer, and for the whole that is humanity. The fates and fortunes of black, white, red, brown, and yellow are intertwined—for better or worse. An aggrandized colony can be a source of positive change for the good of America. Implicit in this colonized reconstruction is achievement of the goals of the colonized—acknowledgement of ethnic history and culture, equity in the application of ethical humanistic justice, and most important, the ultimate control of their own destinies.

There are critical decisions to be made by the colonized community as to which direction it will go: It may continue on the path toward separatism and isolation, or it may, through newly perceived roles, assume a rightful contributing place in the total human society.

MODEL 1
The Process To Intra/Inter Group Black Solidarity

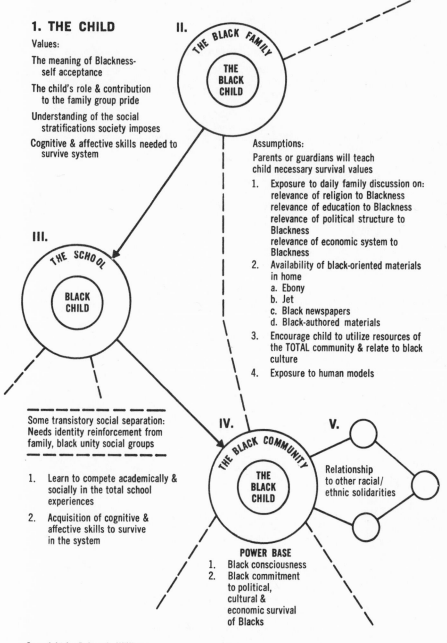

1. THE CHILD

Values:

The meaning of Blackness-
self acceptance

The child's role & contribution
to the family group pride

Understanding of the social
stratifications society imposes

Cognitive & affective skills needed to
survive system

II.

THE BLACK FAMILY

THE
BLACK
CHILD

Assumptions:

Parents or guardians will teach
child necessary survival values

1. Exposure to daily family discussion on:
   relevance of religion to Blackness
   relevance of education to Blackness
   relevance of political structure to
   Blackness
   relevance of economic system to
   Blackness

2. Availability of black-oriented materials
   in home
   a. Ebony
   b. Jet
   c. Black newspapers
   d. Black-authored materials

3. Encourage child to utilize resources of
   the TOTAL community & relate to black
   culture

4. Exposure to human models

III.

THE SCHOOL

BLACK
CHILD

Some transitory social separation:
Needs identity reinforcement from
family, black unity social groups

1. Learn to compete academically &
   socially in the total school
   experiences

2. Acquisition of cognitive &
   affective skills to survive
   in the system

IV.

THE BLACK COMMUNITY

THE
BLACK
CHILD

V.

Relationship
to other racial/
ethnic solidarities

POWER BASE
1. Black consciousness
2. Black commitment
   to political,
   cultural &
   economic survival
   of Blacks

Copyright by Robert L. Williams

CHAPTER TWO

Colonizers at the National, State, and Local Levels

... the President and Congress should have brought in
a national program headed by the President and
ratified by Congress for integration according
to a certain plan. The idea of throwing everybody
together in integrated schools without anybody having
should do it, except the courts seemed to me a very
any idea as to how it would work out, and who
crude and irresponsible proceeding. Walter Lippmann,
Reprinted by permission of *The New Republic*, © 1971,
Harrison-Blaine of New Jersey, Inc.

There are three types of colonizers in American society: *institutional*, *structural*, and *human*. *Institutional* colonizers are those societal systems whose essential framework, characteristics, and mechanisms deny access to power to those outside the existing organization. *Structural* colonizers are the policies and practices derived from executive action of the institution that contribute to maintaining the equilibrium of power distribution, and thus the system of colonization. *Human* colonizers are the individuals whose actions or inactions create the network of structural policies that now entrap the people of the colony. Both structural and human colonizers, like the institutional colonizers described in the first chapter, are the products of a society polluted by racism. There are five structural colonizers that I shall discuss here: the ambiguity of legislative language, lack of well-defined terms, legislative compromises, anti-busing statutes, and the pass-the-buck tactics of state and local governments. All of these structural colonizers are essentially word games with one area of structural colonization depending upon and overlapping another area.

An example of the first of the structural colonizers can be found in the language of the Constitution which prohibits segregation, but does not require integration. The fourteenth amendment prohibits denial of, but does not mandate, equal protection of both Federal and State laws. Section 610 of the 1964 Civil Rights Act clearly states that:

> No person in the United States shall, on the grounds
> of race, creed or national origin, be . . . subject
> to discrimination under any program or
> activity receiving Federal financial assistance.

The policies on School Compliance with Title IV of the same act just as clearly state that "These policies do not require the correction of racial imbalance resulting from private housing patterns."

Structural colonizers need not be positive statements; the lack of a specific statement can be just as devastating. The absence of a clear definition by either Congress or the Supreme Court of what constitutes a segregated school or school system, a desegregated school or school system and an integrated school or school system, is a perfect illustration of this problem.

De facto segregation has never really been defined at the national level, nor has the Supreme Court issued a clear position against the sanctity of northern *de facto* segregated neighborhoods and segregated neighborhood schools. Lower court decisions have provided a set of conditions for *de jure* segregation. Essentially, the state or the local school board must have taken some action with the purpose of segregating. The structural colonizer here is the phrase "with the purpose of segregating." The "purpose" of segregation is *manifest* in all-white schools in all-white neighborhoods that reluctantly receive black students bused in, but oppose any notion of sending their white children across town to the all-black schools.

Also, the action taken by the school system must have, in fact, created or aggravated segregation in the schools under question. The Coleman Report has documented in painstaking detail the academic and social "aggravations" to children attending racially isolated schools.

The third requisite for *de jure* segregation is the existence of current segregation. One has only to observe the composition of pupil populations of individual schools to see that many are not representative of the total pupil population of the community. Most of the minority group children (defined by the Department of Health, Education and Welfare guidelines as black, Indian, oriental, and Spanish surnamed Americans) may be found in a few schools, usually located in the central city. This pattern of racial apartheid may be observed in varying degrees in the north, south, east and west. If we are looking for a "condition of segregation," we need only to observe the concentration patterns of racial groups in selected schools. One may find, to be sure, a sprinkling of minority-group children in scattered peripheral schools. These are the schools to which school boards point with pride as "integrated." Usually such pronouncements are predicated on the presence of two or three minority group pupils enrolled, usually participants in a voluntary transfer program.

A fourth requisite for *de jure segregation* is the existence of a casual relationship between the actions of the school board and the current condition of the school. The presence of all or any one of the conditions may be interpreted as a violation of an individual's guaranteed protection under the Fourteenth Amendment. The Supreme Court established the constitutional right of all children to be protected from discrimination in school admission in its review of Cooper vs Aaron. Further, once such an interpretation of constitutional rights is made, as in Cooper vs Aaron, these rights cannot be nullified by state legislation, state or local executive action, or lower court decisions.

Most definitions of segregation are premised on the presence of *minority* group students; desegregation is seen as achieving racial balance. No part of the definition is based on the presence of *minority* group students. Therefore, the colonizer sees no responsibility for the majority group child or community to share in the desegregation process. It has failed to register on the national mentality that an all-white school in a multi-racial community is just as segregated as the all-black school, or that an all-rich school in a multi-faceted economic community is just as segregated as the all-poor school. Segregation, in the minds of most people, almost always connotes a concentration of minority group pupils in a school. Immediately following is the presumption that there is something wrong with the school, and the cause of the wrongness has to do with the presence of minority children. This sets up a hue and cry for special resources to deal with the "problem"; however, any solution must still keep the children confined to the ghetto school.

A few states and local school boards have issued policies calling for the elimination of racial imbalance. A few courts have issued opinions supporting the prerogative of local districts to achieve racial balance in their schools. However, the colonized community must not fall into the trap of believing that a policy or even actions supporting racial balance is a commitment to integration. The racial balance theory is in itself a racist concept, since it is predicated on the presence of minority group students.

Another structural colonizer is the compromising away of benefits to the colonized community from provisions in legislation introduced in Congress. The initial bills are watered down through political compromises between individuals, who for the most part, appear to place political priorities above the educational welfare of children. The Emergency School Assistance Act at the time of this writing, was still pending. The fact that it became a compromise bill between the Nixon administration and Senator Walter Mondale is significant. Neither the Administration's bill or Mondale's proposal mandated compulsory citywide desegregation. Neither of the bills proposed the involvement of suburban schools in desegregation programs to arrest the increase of racial isolation between city and suburb. Both bills relied on the voluntary aspects of desegregation, with funds being allocated only to those schools meeting the requirements of the Swann Case.

Paul Greenberg, a columnist for Universal Press Syndicate, in the Minneapolis Star of August 12, 1971, summarizes the Nixon administration's lack of commitment to school desegregation. Identified, in parentheses, are the structural colonizers. The Greenberg summary states:

> The President's statement was prompted by a court case in Austin, Texas. But it's difficult to see how the government can justify less busing than ordered by the court there. To quote the reaction of Austin's superintendent of schools, Jack Davidson: "man in White House speaks with forked tongue."

> . . . The district order itself concentrated on minimizing busing, (a structural colonizer) and if the administration really wanted a plan to do that, the Austin plan met those requirements.

> . . .Perhaps the most meretricious part of the statement was the President's insistence that the Emergency School bill now in Congress should "expressly prohibit the expenditure of any of those funds for busing." (a structural colonizer)

> . . . HEW hoped to and came up with an amendment that would forbid the use of any such funds "for the transportation of students to or from schools, whatever the reason might be for such transportation." (a structural colonizer)

Instead of a piece of machinery that has its advantage and disadvantages, the school bus has emerged as the new peril. The president's stand against it is more show than substance: Less than three percent of last year's emergency aid (less than $2 million out of $75 million) went for buses and busing. (a structural colonizer)

... The more emotional a dispute, pershaps the greater need for leaders who will approach it in a rational and flexible way, offering practical solutions instead of fighting the problem. The spectacle of St. Richard going off to fight the yellow dragon may be diverting, but it isn't very helpful.

A more equitable and comprehensive proposal was submitted by Senator Abraham Ribicoff and was overwhelmingly defeated in the House. We can speculate that the bill's defeat was due to its emphasis on the mandatory assignment of white children to predominantly black schools as well as the assignment of black children to predominantly white schools. The clinker was the mandatory assignment of white children, which seems to be the crux of white America's opposition to the desegregation of schools.

The Emergency School Assistance Act and other aid for desegregation, or for the disadvantaged are excellent examples of structural colonization through legislative word games. It appears that local school systems may use Federal monies directed toward desegregation activities for planning or operational programs, but not for busing.

Section 401 of Title IV of the Civil Rights Act (Title IV provides funds for educational programs) reads:

Desegregation means the assignment of students to public schools and within the schools without regard to their race, color, religion, or national origin; but desegregation (here is the great colonizer again) shall not mean the assignment of students to public shools in order to overcome racial imbalance.

If a racially unbalanced school is a segregated school, then it follows that, in order to be desegregated, pupils would need to be assigned with the expressed purpose of overcoming racial imbalance. Contradictions such as these lead one to question the commitment of the federal government to school desegregation. Postures such as President Nixon's proposed amendment to the Emergency School Assistance Bill—that money for busing come from state and local funds—erect formidable barriers to the desegregation of schools. If schools are racially isolated, they are presumably in violation of the laws. It is incumbent upon the local school district to take the necessary steps to meet the provisions of the Fourteenth Amendment to the Constitution. Defiance by national, state, and local leaders does not interfere with, or limit, the authority of court orders to desegregate school systems, nor does it negate the Swann decision, in which the courts reaffirmed the support of local school districts choosing to desegregate schools. Racially isolated schools cannot be desegregated without the mandatory assignment of pupils to other schools beyond their traditional, racially isolated "neighborhoods." Racial imbalance cannot be overcome to any significant degree without the mandatory reassignment of pupils from one school to another. No way!

A fifth colonizer is the collaborative circular conspiracy among national, state, and local government agencies to avoid desegregation. In one round of this racial game playing, the local school board absolves itself of any responsibility for desegregation, stating that it is within the jurisdiction of the state board of education.

The state board of education declines any actions to desegregate in deference to direction from the state legislature. The state legislature takes a conservative posture toward desegregation in deference to its anti-integrationist legislators, or it will take no action until clear guidelines are available and active leadership comes from the Federal government. But the national leadership is remote. The national administration has, by its very inaction, shifted the burden for desegregation back to the states, and the states back to the local school boards.

Certainly some local school boards will use the "lack of funds" position to exonerate themselves from their responsibilities to desegregate school systems. There are a few local and state boards of education that have proclaimed their commitments to the goals of desegregation and integration. But these school boards are faced with dwindling revenue resources and find it increasingly difficult to fulfill commitments to desegregation without additional resources. The cost of busing is most frequently cited as the main reason for opposition to desegregation programs. Districts are faced with the options of re-ordering program priorities using existing available resources or seeking additional revenue from municipal and state governments. Both options are likely to escalate community unrest where there already exists a communications void between the school board and the community. Federal financial support is not only essential, it is imperative. Federal assistance to cover the cost of pupil transportation would remove one more reason for local opposition based on the premise that too much of the local tax dollar is being used for busing. A deletion of the anti-busing provision from the federal guidelines would also be a positive commitment and reinforcement to local school districts attempting to fulfill the promise of the equal protection clause of the Fourteenth Amendment to the Constitution.

Another game playing tactic to evade the implementation of desegregation programs is to appoint a citizen study committee. A local school board or a state board will appoint a group of citizens to "study" the feasibility of desegregation. These sincere citizens will spend many hours without pay researching, analyzing, and exploring alternative plans for desegregation. They will prepare a report of recommendations for the local or state boards of education that will be taken under advisement before being referred to the administrative staff for reworking and resubmission to the boards. Sometimes, to extend the game, new committees are appointed to continue exploration of the findings of the first committee. This is a ruthless colonizer tactic that is destined to backfire, particularly when citizens become involved. Involvement breeds awareness, the antecedent of awakening. As citizens become involved there are oftentimes accompanying changes in their goals, perceptions, and expectations. These citizens may collectively begin to see themselves and the study committee as a decision-making unit in collaboration on an equal basis with the school board and the school administration—a power neither the school board nor school administration is willing to share.

There is a sixth colonizer—it is human. It is the governors, the state superintendents, school boards, and state legislature members who refuse to commit themselves to the desegregation of schools. No state has yet established an agency with the necessary enforcement powers to insure local desegregation. No state has advocated statewide desegregation of the all-white as well as the all-black schools. No state legislature has allocated a significant amount of resources for those school districts attempting desegregation. At the local level, there is a noticeable absence of verbal, written, or financial commitment to two-way citywide desegregation. If school boards have passed resolutions or guidelines advocating desegregation, they have not or could not allocate resources to accomplish their stated goals.

Educational Alternative: If We Really Mean To Desegregate Schools: A Model And A Method. Dealing with segregated schools is analogous to dealing with a disease—the school must be systematically analyzed, diagnosed as segregated, and then a remedy must be prescribed. A segregated school is a polluted school. It is a product of the most deadly of all pollution—the pollution of racism.

A distinction should be made at this juncture between the desegregation of schools, the integration of schools, and racial balance. Desegregation of schools is a process having to do with a quantitative physical mixing of pupils and faculties of various racial and economic backgrounds, bringing them into a learning environment for a definite length of time. Desegregation *precedes* integration. Integration refers to qualitative affective relationships between persons together in a common setting. A social scientist might describe these relationships as positive valances or warm feelings of acceptance. Educators describe the sum of these warm feelings of acceptance as an atmosphere of mutual trust and respect among the students, faculty, parents, and community. Integration follows desegregation and is essentially a long range ideal. It is possible to desegregate a school without integrating. A school is not integrated (I doubt if it can even be called desegregated,) if there are segregated all-white and all-black classes within the same building. A school is not integrated if the black faculty members are relegated to lower level assignments. Nor is a school integrated if the black students do not enjoy full participation in activities they enjoyed in their all-black school. Racial balance is a discriminatory concept premised on the presence of minority group children in a school. It places the burden for integrating on the shoulders of the minority group child.

We now turn to the question of how a segregated school may be diagnosed. Most diagnoses begin with a definition of a disease; however, individuals and groups at the national, state and local levels are reluctant to come to grips with such a definition for segregation. These individuals know full well that once they arrive at a definition, a commitment of intent is revealed, and a strategy to action is implied. In order to avoid or delay action to desegregate schools, one avoids a definition. When a definition is finally arrived at and applied to each of the schools in the district, it becomes clear which are racially isolated.

Racial isolation in schools must be eradicated if the colonizing cycle is to be broken—poor education leads to poor jobs; poor jobs lead to poor housing; poor housing leads to poor neighborhoods; poor neighborhoods lead to poor schools; poor schools complete the circle—poor education. Obviously the place to begin breaking this self-perpetuating dehumanizing cycle is the schools. To wait for housing patterns to change would be to wait too long.

The model presented at the end of this chapter (Model 2) is based on a definition of a segregated school as one which fails to reflect the racial composition of the total community. The model is based on the assumptions that (1) schools, reflecting the dynamics of society, are moving towards greater racial isolation; (2) that integrated education cannot be achieved in racially isolated schools; (3) that a relationship exists between racial stratification and socio-economic status; (4) that social class milieu as well as race are significant variables affecting educational achievement; (5) that desegregation is a two way street involving all racial/economic groups in a community; and finally, (6) that desegregation of schools assumes pupil transportation from one point to another. The recommended steps for using the model are (1) to determine the racial ratio (black/white, and majority-group/minority-group) of the total community using local census figures and school sight counts; (2) determine from the Health, Education and Welfare data (H.E.W.) or Aid to Families With Dependent Children data (A.F.D.C.), the economic range of the total community; (3) determine the racial ratio of the school under diagnosis by using the bi-modal black/white, and majority-group/minority group grid; (4) now impose a sliding scale value for racial-economic groupings, indicating a floor below which no racial-economic group percentage would be allowed to fall, and a ceiling above which no racial-economic group would be allowed to exceed. (This model illustration is based on a hypothetical school/community racial composition of 90 percent white population and 10 percent black population.)

The sliding scale indicates the "danger zone" floors and ceilings with shaded areas of the Z.O.R.—zone of reflection. The shaded area constitutes a warning zone, the point at which corrective action should be taken to prevent the school under diagnosis from becoming more segregated. The black/minority group range on the bi-modal grid is 5 percent to 35 percent. The white/majority group range is 65 percent to 95 percent. In this case, no school would be allowed to exceed more than 35 percent black/minority group pupils and 95 percent white/majority group pupils; nor would any school be allowed to fall below 5 percent black/minority group pupils and 65 percent white/majority group pupils. Economically, the ceilings would apply equally to all racial groups. A school with more than 35 percent of its pupils below the H.E.W. poverty standard would be considered segregated. A school with more than 95 percent of its pupils above the H.E.W. poverty standard would also be considered segregated.

The model is proposed as a working model for diagnosing a school as segregated. Obviously it is not applicable to every local school situation nor can it instantly reverse three hundred years of individual and institutional racism. It is, however, a model and a method capable of being adapted to urban school systems.

Within the behavioral context, this model describes a desegregated school and further delineates the conditions and the criteria for assessment. It is a behavioral accountability mechanism. We may note the three conditional components of a behaviorally stated objective:

Condition: Given—the racial composition of the total community as determined through local census or school sight count; and the economic range of the entire community, as determined from H.E.W. poverty line or A.F.D.C. data.

Criteria: Ascertain a sliding scale for racial-economic groupings, indicating a floor below which no racial economic group percentage will be allowed to fall, and a ceiling which no racial-economic group will be allowed to exceed. No school would be allowed to exceed more than 35% black/minority-group pupils and 95% white pupils; or no school would be allowed to fall below 5% black pupils and 65% white pupils. No school would be allowed to have more than 35% of its pupils below the poverty standard, or 95% of its pupils above the poverty standard.

Observable Act: In this case, observe the profile of the enrollment within the attendance units in the district, and compare that enrollment profile with the criteria.

Finally, this model, as opposed to the one way minority dispersal racial balance models, emphasizes equity in pupil sharing. Further, it places responsibility on the total community —white, black, yellow, red, and tan—to share in the process of desegregation. Desegregation is the first step in the process of integration. It must not become an end in itself. It must be accompanied by vigorous faculty in-service education and extensive community participation.

What are the implications for a school system adapting such a model? This model might change the patterns of pupil placement for both majority group and minority group pupils, or change the boundary attendance area patterns; it could very well affect changes in building facility construction or arrangement and site selections for placement of new buildings. Acceptance of the model could increase the majority group community's concern about education in the minority group community and bring about a closer working relationship between minority group and majority group communities.

Conflict and confrontation are possibilities if a school system implements such a model. Adoption of the model could affect the goals of decentralization and local community control, or bring about conflict with those advocating black and white separatism. Hopefully, a desegregation/integration process based on this model would involve representatives from all racial-ethnic-economic levels, so that communication and the desegregation process would be a self-renewal experience for the colony.

Desegregation is not an easy process, and the colonized community must not expect help from the colonizer. Colonized people must come to understand that the colonizer, by virtue of his life experience, will have a limited vision for integration, and is bound by his role-position outside the colony, to defend that which he believes to be a normative goal—preserving the status quo. Desegregation/integration, unfortunately, is not a perceived goal of the colonizer.

Desegregation must be achieved in the schools in spite of the colonizer. We cannot wait for housing patterns to change.

MODEL 2
Desegregating A School Racially And Economically

Definitive Premise
The model is based on the definition of a segregated school as one which fails to reflect the common heritage of the total school district's school population.

Steps in Using the Model
1. Determine the district's racial ratio.
2. Determine each school's racial ratio.
3. Determine the Zone of Reflection (ZOR)
4. Chart the school to be diagnosed.
5. Superimpose chart on the model.

Assumptions Underlying the Model
1. Schools reflecting the dynamics of society are moving toward greater racial division.
2. A relationship exists between racial stratification and socio-economic status.
3. Integrated education cannot be achieved in segregated schools.
4. Social class milieu as well as race are significant variables affecting pupil educational achievement.
5. Desegregation a "two-way" street will require pupil transportation.

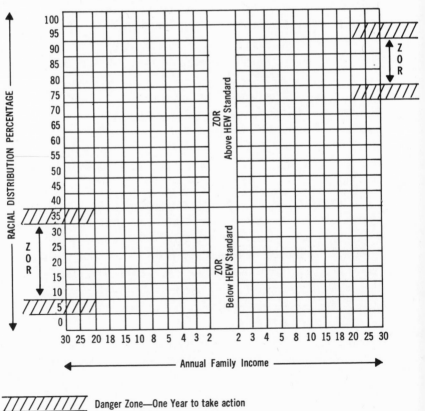

Danger Zone—One Year to take action

Those who are naive enough to believe that housing patterns will change have only to read the report of the Advisory Commission on Crime and Civil Disorders. Those who advocate desegregated neighborhoods as the *sine qua non* to desegregated schools are asking that colonized people wait out their lives as colonized subjects. Housing patterns are becoming more racially isolated by the day, in large measure due to federal complicity. FHA loans have facilitated the exodus of whites from the inner city to the suburbs; FHA low income housing programs have served to perpetuate racial and economic segregation. The guidelines for the program make it easier for more Whites than Blacks to purchase homes in white suburbs, while Blacks have been restricted by financial qualifications in the program to purchasing old homes in a decaying central city.

However, in attempting to desegregate schools we are attempting to treat a symptom instead of curing the disease. The disease, of course, is racism. But the desegregation of schools is a major step in the process of curing the disease, and in doing so, it may just drive the first wedge into the wall surrounding the colony.

CHAPTER THREE

Schools of the Colony

Any discussion of a school that serves colonized children must consider three dimensions: its profile, its philosophy and its people.

There is an ever widening gulf in America's urban areas between schools attended by colonized children and those attended by the children of the colonizer. There is a disproportionate number of low achieving students attending schools in low income and ghetto neighborhoods. Evidence presented in one urban school desegregation suit showed that in the twelve school buildings designated as segregated, 34 percent of the teachers were new, 48 percent had less than three years experience and only 17 percent of the teachers had ten or more years of experience. By contrast, in twenty other school buildings in the same district, only 9 percent of the teachers were new, and nearly 50 percent had at least ten years of experience. The ghetto schools have older, inferior plant facilities, high teacher turnover rates, low faculty morale, and, possibly most damaging, a lack of parent/community trust in its overall educational effectiveness. These conditions seriously impair the ability of the school to provide equal (or even adequate) educational opportunities for colonized children. Many schools, which might not be technically segregated, use a bell curve of ability distribution to group pupils into classes on the basis of I.Q. scores, thus achieving inbuilding segregation.

The bell curve is usually used by educators to represent performance on a test. When classes are grouped solely on the basis of I.Q. scores, the bell curve can become a structural colonizer. The I.Q. tests devised by whites using white vocabularies and learning experiences and based on white standards are inherently unfair to minority children. A more comprehensive definition of intelligence is one that considers the effects of pre- and post-natal environment, the specific cognitive and learning style of the student, and genetic considerations. The concern is not so much with definitions of intelligence as with the educational policies resultng from them. For those who believe that intelligence is a function of a racial genetic base, the bell curve of I.Q. scores merely reinforces an educational model based on ability distribution—the inequity ability model—because after all, nature created the inequities in the first place! Any model based on individual ability performance levels becomes invalid when it is translated into arbitrary assumptions about groups of people, particularly when these assumptions are based on the emotionalism of racism. The danger in the educational system comes when the racist-based assumptions become expectations, and when classroom practices are arranged to fulfill the expectations. Concepts such as "equal educational opportunities." "compensatory education," and "enrichment programs" connote the presumed needs of colonized children.

The classroom practice of sorting and screening on the basis of I.Q. does untold damage to the self-image of the colonized child. An internalized negative self-image causes him to reduce his level of aspiration. This, in turn, retards the learning process. The cycle does not end here. The classroom teacher, sensing the lowered aspirations of the colonized pupil, makes the mistake of lowering his expectations for the pupil. The pupil fulfills the lowered teacher expectation. The educational standards of the classroom fall; the educational standards of the school fall; the morale of the faculty falls; the pupils' pride in the school falls; the parents' and finally, the community's esteem for the school falls.

The inequity ability model is related to the attitudes of colonizer-oriented teachers and their teaching behavior. There is little question that far too many educators come to the colonized school with preconceived assumptions about colonized children's values. A study by Groff of high teacher turnover showed some 40 percent of teachers making references to "peculiarities" in ghetto children. A study by Herriot and St. John showed teachers in ghetto schools showing less interest in their pupils where advance classroom preparation was the criteria. Low expectations for colonized children was cited as a value of middle-class teachers in Strom's study. Studies by David and Dollard showed low-income children receiving fewer rewards in the classroom regardless of ability. A study by David and Lang showed that negative teacher attitudes contributed directly to lowered pupil achievement and lowered pupil self-esteem. Research findings by Gage suggest rather clearly that teachers in colonized schools hold different attitudes toward culturally different children, and further, that these attitudes relate directly to their classroom teaching behaviors.

At another level of classroom practice, the bell curve indirectly dictates classroom teacher practices when a teacher looks at a profile of next year's class and thinks, "a small percentage of my pupils are at the upper end of the distribution. These will be my A students . . . a few will be at the bottom of the distribution . . . I will have to keep an eye on these . . ." Such a teacher unwittingly is setting an expectation for a pupil population he has never seen. Further, he has imposed on his pupils the most devastating of all colonizer values—the value of "perfectionism" and it's educational corollary, the "perfect" score of 100. The classroom becomes a colonizer, a vertical hierarchy of "climbers." The colonized child soon discovers that he is without the necessary climber values and climber skills (verbal ability skills as defined by colonizer standards) to compete successfully with his classmates with more favorable pre- and post-natal environments. Thus, he learns early in his educational career the frustration that comes with daily classroom failure.

What is needed is a new ability model predicated on the assumption that every child entering school has enough ability (barring irreversible pre- or post-natal injury) to achieve the minimum cognitive skills needed for educational and social survival. Such a model presumes the behavioral identification and assimilation of these skills as the primary educational goal for colonized children. This would preclude classroom grouping based solely on I.Q. scores and negative teacher expectations derived from a bell curve mentality.

Another example of educational practices being created to fulfill expectancies based on racist assumptions is the case of the black administrator. The black administrator of the seventies has the dubious distinction of being an "instant" administrator. The overnight promotion of Blacks to administrative positions is a direct result of the racial riots in the summer of 1964. Prior to the riots there were very few Blacks in administrative or supervisory positions; now school boards point with pride to "Blacks at every level of administration in our school system." Yet, there are less than fifty black superintendents in the nation; of the school systems in cities with more than 100,000 population, only two have black superintendents; few Blacks are principals of desegregated schools. The reason often given for the absence of black administrators is the "lack of qualified candidates." When school boards see applicants for new or vacated positions, they do not expect Blacks to be qualified, so despite the list of highly qualified Blacks seeking assignments maintained by the Afro-American Educator Association placement bureau, they rarely find any qualified candidates.

The caucuses among black educators at national conferences have come to be the vehicle by which black educators analyze their common exploited plight. Too many black administrators perceive their positions in a negative light, an overabundance of pressures wthout the power to change the situations causing pressure—overworked and underpaid, over-exposed and under-promoted. Most black administrators expressed concern over the negative connotations implied by their job titles—"administrative assistant to," "administrative aide," "executive aide." All expressed concern that these assignments are only advisory positions, non-decision-making roles, without power to affect the educational destinies of colonized children. Most black administrators are on the lowest rung of the power heirarchy (span of control and size of budget), most agreed that they were discovered and promoted as stop gap measures to act as a buffer between dissatisfied, frustrated minority communities and the school system.

Many black administrators often feel alienated from their colleagues. If he is effective, he is likely to be seen by them as a threat. The struggle for power is usually responsible for this perception. (Henry contends that friction between departments is directly proportional to their power and the degree of overlap between them.) His alienation is further aggravated by his political adeptness at carrying out his job responsibilities without compromising his commitment to the educational liberation of colonized children. He must master the game playing skills of the colonizer in order to effect change in the educational policy of the district. In the final analysis, the black administrator's power, whether he is a principal or a superintendent, is in his support from the black community. This support could be his most effective weapon to facilitate change from his precarious position.

The existence of racism at both school and central administration levels presents educators with tasks of the highest priority. Educators must exercise vigilance that racist classroom educational practice deriving from invalid assumptions about the life chances of colonized children must not come into existence, and those now in existence (classroom grouping based solely on I.Q. scores, for example) must be abolished. Professional personnel in the system must be re-educated so that negative teacher expectations of colonized children's performances do not become self-fulfilling prophecies. Recruitment and personnel policies must be scrutinized to guard against tokenism or quotaism, and black administrators must be given real power in order to achieve the goal of educational liberation for colonized children.

Educational Alternative: The Spinning Wheel School

A proposed alternative to the present ghetto school is what I choose to call the *Spinning Wheel School* (see model, page 64). The school's name derives from its dynamic lateral team teaching/learning approach in which groupings of pupils move laterally around team faculty members for specified, though flexible, time periods. The students are grouped on the basis of individual behavioral performance and behaviorally demonstrated learner needs. This is a contrast to present grouping techniques based on I.Q. Four heterogenously derived groupings move around a team of four specialists in four learning areas: family living and cultural skills, communications skills, computational skills, and marketable survival skills. The groupings are flexible, varying in size according to student movement between groups. Each grouping is in a specialized learning area for flexible periods of time. The human element may very well be the most important variable in determining the success or failure of the wheel school. Hence, the question of school size becomes important. The pupil/teacher ratio for each lateral team should not exceed fifty pupils for five faculty team members. There may be as many as thirty lateral team units comprising a single wheel school.

A school day might be divided into seven one-hour periods Under such a time schedule, the total pupil population would spend the first period with one of the learning specialists in a nonstructured, everyday life-oriented situation. The student might read the morning newspaper or watch educationally oriented television programs such as "Sesame Street," the "Electric Company" or "The Today Show." The idea is to expose the colonized child to experiences which might not be available in his home.

The second period of the day might find all four groups in computational skill classes. Pupils will move at different levels within a given group. This might be accomplished by breaking the general computational objectives down into individually prescribed instructional tasks of relatively short duration. Many of these tasks can be directly related to everyday experiences.

The third period might find all groups in marketable survival skills classes. Here the class would be oriented to exploratory experiences, such as field trips to career centers, so that the student might observe at first hand successful members of the colonized community, such as the electrician. Local merchants businessmen, and skilled workers might be brought in to share their vocational experiences with the students. An Indian-American poet might be brought in to share his experiences as an Indian-American and as a poet. Boys might be exposed to cooking and sewing crafts at the same time girls are exposed to auto mechanics and simple carpentry so that they both would have survival skills once they left the family unit.

The fourth period would be set aside for lunch and recreation. Here is an excellent opportunity for faculty team members to broaden their social relationships with the colonized children. Again, there is a contrast to the present neighborhood school with its separate student and faculty dining facilities. An after lunch walk around the block chat between a faculty member and his students has unlimited potential for building positive human relationships.

Family living-cultural skills might be the subject of the fifth period. Here the colonized family as a unit is enforced. Educators must not attempt to alter in a negative way the deeply enculturated values of the colonized child. They must not belittle the cultural patterns he brings from home. Instead, the educator must reinforce those cultural values already instilled in the child. To be successful, any educational process must utilize and build on the experiences and resources of the learner.

The sixth period would be devoted to communications skills. The daily newspaper might be used as a lesson guide. The students might be provided with opportunities to listen and speak in various ethnic idioms. This is one way to reinforce those cultural communications patterns the colonized child brings to the learning setting. However, the educator must guard against substituting "ghettoese," or other ethnic language patterns for the standardized language pattern. It is imperative that colonized children are taught to communicate in the idiom of the colonizer if the child is to acquire the necessary skills to transcend the conditions of colonization. Conversely, the educator must guard against destroying the cultural communications patterns that are the heritage of the colonized child, they, too, are a survival skill.

The seventh period of the day might be put to use as a winding down period for the school day. It might also be used as a reinforcement period in which the student is reinforced for having successfully accomplished mutually agreed to tasks.

Since many ghetto children enter school without the cognitive skill readiness necessary for learning, they invent defense mechanisms to protect an ego conditioned to failure. Constant misbehavior, inattention, "mouthing off" to faculty members, habitual tardiness, and absenteeism are familiar examples of such defense mechanisms. The guidance counselor, the fifth team member of a wheel school grouping, can do much to minimize negative behavior from his position in the "center" of the wheel. The counselor would be mobile; his office would be wherever a problem would arise. Because the guidance counselor would be working with a limited, manageable number of students instead of the two to three hundred clients that a counselor usually has, personal relationships could be initiated and maintained. Drawing on these relationships, counselors would be able to provide options and alternatives not ordinarily possible in a traditional setting. The student could, as an option, "get off the lateral merry-go-round" to concentrate on a particular subject area, or the student might be free to move within the wheel at will, or to exit from a learning area into the guidance service area.

Not only the counselor, but the entire wheel school faculty, will work to gain the confidence of the child and, of course, work to sustain the relationship. The philosophic basis of the wheel school is to accept the colonized student as he is—to love and respect the essence of the person—and then to accept his dress, his hair style and his language patterns. Accept his language style, but watch his choice of language! A team member for the wheel school must hold an abiding faith in children and their abilities to transcend the conditions of colonization. Classroom objectives must be constantly re-evaluated and adjusted in light of the needs of the student. A faculty member must believe that the colonized child has a contribution to make to the larger society, and that colonized children will need compensatory services at times to help them towards self-actualization. This means the faculty member must be compensatory/proportionate-closing-of-the-gap oriented. The faculty team member in a wheel school is more a facilitator of media and methods to the learning process than he is a teacher. Learning becomes more of a student responsibility as a consequence. The educator team member of the wheel school must be relatively free of hang-ups about the genetic basis of intelligence. He must be comfortable with the position that I.Q. is more relevant to assumptions about class than about education.

The wheel school must be accountable to the colonized community. Specifically, there must be behaviorial accountability for the performance and achievement of the children. Accountability in the wheel school must show a three-way involvement among the pupils, the parents and the faculty team members. This three-way accountability can be possible only when there are clearly stated, achievable behavioral goals at the system, school, and classroom levels. Schools will continue to be attacked as inefficient and ineffective until educational goals are clearly defined, and measurable behavioral objectives derived from these goals are clearly stated.

The lack of clearly stated educational goals is not an accident. Many educators are reluctant to define exactly what they are attempting to do, or admit how they intend to measure success or failure. Consequently, programs are funded without any evidence of their effectiveness. Educators will sometimes comment that certain classroom activities are worthwhile, that some materials are better than others, that one teacher or one school is better than another. The truth of the matter is that we have never established clear criteria for establishing or refuting the validity of such claims. Our assessments have been (except laboratory controlled experiments) based on intuitive speculation about students and the learning process. It is impossible for the average educator to substantiate evidence of any educational accomplishments because no assessable goals had been stated. Educator Donald Christensen asserts there can be little claim of accomplishment when there is no expression of what the student will be able to do at the end of a specified learning period. At best, all that can be claimed are vague "perceived" changes in learner behavior as measured subjectively on standardized tests. Obviously, these have little relevance to colonized children. These tests show little more than a dubious relationship between the actual pupil performance on a given instrument and the classroom activities of the teacher. If on the other hand, the classroom teacher can state clearly what behavior the pupil will be expected to demonstrate by the end of the fourth week after completing lessons X, Y, and Z, there can be little question about the progress of the pupil's educational achievement. What is needed in education, particularly in the colonized school, is the statement of educational goals.

Educational goals must be clearly stated in behavioral language naming specific observable acts of pupil behavior to be expected as direct results of instructional activities. The formulation of educational goals for a school system, a school, and a classroom must include the involvement of the community, for the success of an educational program will be in proportion to the community support it receives.

A clearly stated set of behavioral objectives must be formulated from the stated educational goal. A behavioral objective consists of three components: The *Conditions*—those circumstances that permits the end behavior to be observed; the *Criteria*—the guide by which a determination is made as to whether the objective is met; and the *Behavior*—the observable act, or the observable consequences of the act.

An example of a behaviorally stated objective for a computational skills class might be stated as follows:

> *Assignment:* Given 15 items consisting of four, three digit numerals arranged in columns (the condition); add the columns and write (observable outcome) the sum at the bottom of each column; complete the task in twelve minutes, with not more than two incorrect totals (criteria).

An assignment for a lesson in communications skills might be:

> *Assignment:* Given the written accounts on police brutality incidents as published from August 1 through September 1 (condition), write (behavior) a 200 word statement within forty minutes (criteria) stating what you would do if you were Mayor of this city.

Behavioral objectives at the classroom level may be made relevant by tailoring the materials to the interests of the class as suggested by the above communications assignment. The faculty team member, for motivational purposes, may, in collaboration with his students, develop classroom behavioral objectives. The learner is likely to support that which has helped to plan.

The formulation of system-wide objectives for an entire school district is accomplished in much the same manner. The community must be involved from the beginning in the determination of educational goals and objectives. (Educators no longer find it feasible to try to develop objectives in isolation from the community.) Community involvement can start with the establishment of a school/community educational task force. The task force should identify system-wide educational goals and also the behavior required of students, parents and school personnel in order to accomplish the system-wide goals. The task force would study sample groups, noting what teacher performances are required to elicit behavior that appears to fulfill the defined educational goals. These performances would then be outlined and step-by-step objectives would be defined. Educators, again with the help of the community, would prepare instructional methods and materials designed to bring about the behavior delineated in the objectives. This is one way of involving the community while at the same time laying the groundwork for a three-way accountability mechanism.

A commitment by a school system to system-wide objectives is an affirmation of its intent to be accountable to the community it serves. Without behavioral criteria with which to assess the success or failure of a school, education will continue to be the cause of rising dropout rates in colonized schools, high illiteracy rates in the adult population of the colonized communities and social disorders in the colony where youth have more idle time than marketable skills. Reluctance to adopt a policy that would make a district accountable for the education provided should be a cause of concern in any community, but especially in the colonized community. Militancy in the colonized community is on the increase. The colonized community can no longer be accused of passivity. Colonized parents are demanding greater involvement in decisions affecting the destinies of their children. They are concerned with the operation of the schools, the hiring and firing of personnel, the relevancy of curriculum, budget and salaries of teachers and administrators—all issues affecting the destinies of their children. Parents are especially concerned over the increasing numbers of incompetent teachers who find their way into the classrooms of colonized children. Central to the concern is the process of evaluation of teachers and the kind of rewards that are the consequences of this evaluation. The colonized community wants evaluation of teachers based on performance—how much and how well they teach children. Some professional teacher organizations, and educators in general, oppose a salary schedule based on teacher performance. They claim that there is no accurate method of evaluation that would take into account individual learner differences. A school system that utilizes system-wide behavioral objectives, in which the focus is on the behavior of the learner, could facilitate positive resolution of this nagging issue.

The connection of reward to performance has special implications for education. Once the desired result of an educational experience is stated in a manner that can be assessed behavioraly there can be little question as to whether or not the task has been accomplished. Those professionals responsible for successes should be rewarded. Where the learners consistently fail to achieve the stated educational goals, the adults responsible must share the blame. I am speaking of parents as well as educators and pupils.

Education must monitor its own ranks if it is to maintain its status as a profession. It must not be threatened or frightened by performance objectives, merit pay, and accountability. Accountability is maintained in other professions through practices such as quality control in industry, rigid bar examinations before entry into the practice of law, and promotions on the basis of production efficiency throughout the entire economic system. The establishment of behavioral objectives at system, school building, and classroom level can help a school system to better monitor how certain administrators, teachers, instructional methods and materials are influencing the achievement of children. The use of behavioral objectives can help to better justify to the community those practices and materials that are most effective in achieving system-wide or classroom objectives. The school district is then in a better position for rallying political and economic community support for its efforts.

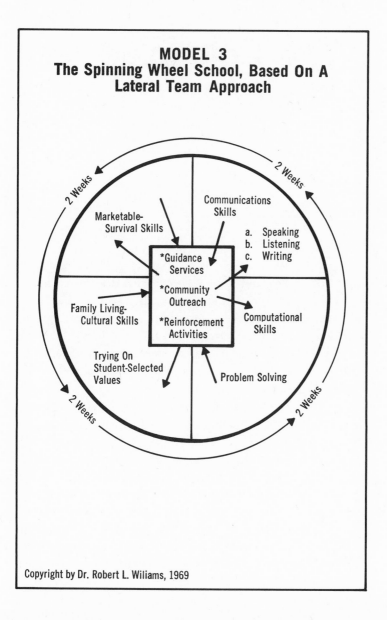

**MODEL 3
The Spinning Wheel School, Based On A
Lateral Team Approach**

2 Weeks

2 Weeks

Communications
Skills

Marketable-
Survival Skills

a. Speaking
b. Listening
c. Writing

*Guidance
Services

*Community
Outreach

Family Living-
Cultural Skills

Computational
Skills

*Reinforcement
Activities

Trying On
Student-Selected
Values

Problem Solving

2 Weeks

2 Weeks

CHAPTER FOUR

The Colonized Pupil

Colonization breeds conditions of pre-natal and post-natal deprivation. Too often such conditions destine colonized children to educational failure before they ever see the inside of a classroom. The social, economic, and political systems in America have perpetuated these conditions through a failure to provide adequate remedial or preventive programs. We cannot lay the blame on any one system; all must collectively share the blame.

Poverty, malnutrition and unbelievably crowded living quarter are the usual environment of the colony. Research studies have substantiated many of the effects of adverse pre-natal environment on children. Malnutrition during pregnancy is believed to be related to debilitating physiological effects on the developing fetus. Susceptibility of pregnant mothers to certain diseases is believed to be related to vitamin deficiencies. These conditions of deprivation are believed to contribute to intellectual retardation in colonized children.

The post-natal environment of the colony holds little hope

of betterment. Unemployment and under-employment are major structural colonizers. Black unemployment is more than double white unemployment. Employment rates are higher for white high school drop-outs than for black high school graduates. But post-natal deprivation is not exclusive to black America. Of some ten million colonized children in America, about two-thirds of them are white. Most of the housing occupied by America's first Americans, the American Indian, is below national health and safety standards. Some seventy-five percent of Spanish-speaking American children struggle for educational survival in classrooms where English is the only language. These are a few of many colonizing conditions allowed to exist while the world's most affluent nation allocates over one-half of its national budget for military spending, but less than sixteen percent for health, education, and welfare programs. The message to the colonized community is all to clear: colonized children are treated differently than colonizer children. Such differential treatment has without a doubt had immeasurable adverse effects on colonized children. James Baldwin in *Fire the Next Time,* underscores the destructive power of post-natal deprivation of the colonized black child: "Long before the black child perceives this difference and even longer before he understands it, he has begun to be controlled by it." (James Baldwin, *Fire the Next Time,* p. 40, Dial Press). Perceptions such as Baldwin's take on a special significance when we know that there are thousands of malnourished black children on federally subsidized southern farms. The validity of Baldwin's assertion is affirmed by the controlling effects of northern welfare-oriented ghettoes on black colonized people. But observations and perceptions are only part of the story.

Research findings on intelligence have brought into the open many of the devastating consequences of racism, particularly as it affects the intellectual capacities of colonized children. Racism is the underlying theme of recently released studies and position papers on I.Q. The debate rages among educators, and the philosophic polarizations resulting from such debates underscore America's malady, the pollution of racism. The subject of race and I.Q. is a great catalyst for precipitating human interdisciplinary socio-political alignments. Sociologist liberals side with the environmentalists. The I.Q.-from-genes proponents find company in the racists. It has been scientifically established that genes control the size of the body, the shape of the nose, the texture of the hair, the color of the skin. I need only say two words, "Mendel" and "peas" and you will nod sagely and murmur "ah yes" and accept, unthinkingly, wholeheartedly, yet without understanding, the principles of the genetic heredity of physical characteristics. Moynihan, Jensen and Hernstein in their research studies have attempted to pick up a torch that Gregor Mendel was wise enough to throw down. They have attempted to prove through statistics, I.Q. scores, SES levels, control groups, reading ability, and psychological theories, that black children are genetically inferior to white children; that genes, not environment, not nutrition, not educational stimuli, that genes are the determinators of intelligence.

Educators, social scientists, psychologists, and lay citizens discuss the I.Q. scores of black children comparing them with the I.Q. scores of white children. But today's controversy over I.Q. is more than just a conflict between environmentalists and geneticists. Racism and elitist assumptions about race are without a doubt the basis for much of the interest in research findings on I.Q. Racist inferences are sometimes extrapolated from findings to validate the racial superiority of a given group. White racists sometimes defend the genetic basis of intelligence using as a base of reference a study by Shuey that concluded: "On the average, blacks test about one standard deviation (15 I.Q. points) below the average white population." Black separatists sometimes argue the environmentalist position citing a World War II study showing that Minnesota Blacks performed better on the army I.Q. tests than did Mississippe Whites. Both groups miss three crucial points:

A.   I.Q. is a measurement describing the performance of

an individual, on a given instrument, at a given time, based on specific criteria.

B.   I.Q. instruments, by and large, have been developed on the cultural norms of Whites, developed almost exclusively by Whites, and standardized on the performance of Whites, for the benefit of Whites.

C.   Whites in American have had a longer period of conditioning to perform on these verbally oriented instruments.

Too often, such nationally acclaimed studies published in nationally acclaimed journals project the colonized pupil in a negative light. One study concluded that upper status black children averaged some 2.6 I.Q. points below the lower status Whites. I do not take issue with the statistic. The study, however, affirms another reality of racism in America: lower-class Whites have had better opportunities for conditioning to perform on verbal instruments than upper-class Blacks. The black male adult today must have between one and three years of college before he can expect to earn as much in his lifetime as his white counterpart with less than eight years of schooling. The black children cited in the study might very well have been products of upper-class families, but these were likely first generation upper-class families. Their lower status white counterparts were descendants of two to three generations conditioned to verbally oriented education—three generations of conditioning to exercising mental capacities.

The studies of Jensen and Hernstein attempt to give an academic cloak of respectability to the white racist mentality which asserts that one race is genetically superior to another. They conveniently disregard factors such as the innate bias of white middle-class created tests, physical environment, vitamin deficiency, social conditions and inadequate educational techniques. Studies refuted the conclusions of Jensen and Hernstein have largely been ignored. Neither the *Atlantic Monthly* nor the *Harvard Review* have given significant coverage to the Milwaukee project, directed by Dr. Rick Heber, or

Dr. William Rohwer's paper, "Learning, Race and School Success."

In the Milwaukee Project, Dr. Heber found that the reason for the unusually high concentration of apparently low I.Q. children in slum areas is the low I.Q. parent residing in the slum environment rather than the environment itself. He also proved, as did Dr. Richard Crutchfield of Berkeley, that intervention with creative educational stimuli and techniques can arrest and reverse the retardation process of low-income black children. Dr. Rohwer, in several studies, deals with the question of school success as a variable more directly related to ethnicity, SES and I.Q. rather than on the ability to learn. He hypothesizes learning as a variable of cognitive style. His model, which involves creative conceptualization training in an interval between a pre- and a post-test, implies that for low SES students care should be taken to provide ample opportunities for acquiring information and skills missed because of inadequate early environmental experience. Some studies overemphasize the superior performance of colonized black children in motor skills. Such studies invariably proclaim Blacks to have higher scores than Whites in motor skills. The inference is that there is some natural ability peculiar to Blacks. The presumption of superior motor ability and inferior mental ability is racist, remindful of Cleaver's piercing analysis of racist mentality. "The Black is perceived as the supermasculine, the mindless beast, and the White, the omnipotent administrator, the great thinker."

Every citizen concerned with the survival of colonized children should study carefully the materials relative to the intellectual capacities of colonized children. Too often such literature and findings are laden with racist myths and racist inferences. The colonized parent and the educator of colonized children should consider such research findings valid only when they can be conducted in culturally fair racism free environments—an ideal whose time has yet to come.

The common denominator of all the studies is an educational intervention based on the learning style of the learner, not the teaching style of the teacher. A variety of educational stimuli and pedigogical alternatives can counteract the retarding effects of the colony environment and can break the cyclic process of low I.Q., low achievement, low income. As to the I.Q. capacity of an entire race being based totally on genetic principles rather than environmental conditions, Mendel would have been the first to admit that even his purest strains of peas would have been dismal failures if they were denied water or sunshine. Children cannot learn in an environment that, for them is not conducive to learning. Educators might take heed of another well-known fact— no two snowflakes are ever exactly alike. If we accept this, why can we not accept the theory that no two children learn in precisely the same way. Therefore, educational achievement in black children can be greatly increased by providing the right educational environment and an individually tailored pedigogical approach that considers the learner's individual cognitive style.

The colonized pupil, to overcome certain conditions of pre-natal and post-natal deprivation, must be provided early childhood education programs. Substantial evidence to date suggests that approximately eighty percent of a child's intelligence is developed by the age of six. Unfortunately, most of the early childhood programs today serve non-colonized middle-class children. This suggests that there is a belief among many parents that intelligence can be modified through environmental experiences, and further, such experiences can and often produce cumulative effects, leading to improved pupil school achievement.

Every colonized pupil should be provided a relevant education. What is a relevant education for a colonized child? A relevant education is that education which enables him to firstly, achieve a positive self-image, and secondly, effectively deal with the system that oppresses him. Such an education enables him to enhance his life-style and improve his life-chances. The question of what enhances a life-style and improves life-chances can, in the final analysis, only be answered by a colonized student. A guidepost should be noted: relevance of an education is relative to a condition. Relevant education for the colonized child must be relative to his goal for liberation from the conditions that oppress him.

What are the essential components of a relevant educational program for colonized children? It must include program offerings in early childhood readiness, cultural-esthetic development, basic communications skills, basic computational skills, and adult-marketable skills. The community must demand from school boards serving colonized children that these components be enmeshed into the total educational program, and that these components are accessible to every child. Further, there must be assurance that these components are accountable in explicit behavioral objectives at the system-wide level, at the school level, and at the classroom level for the teacher and the pupil. Only when these are achieved can there be specific accountability from the school, to the parent and the community about the performance of colonizer children.

Educational alternative: Early Childhood Education for Colonized Children. A relevant early childhood education program for colonized children must include four interlocking and overlapping structural learning environments—the home, an early childhood center, the school, and a community reinforcement activities center. Such a program must be based on a continuous learning philosophy. This will mean pupil involvement almost 16 hours a day, seven days a week, 52 weeks a year, from early childhood through adult education.

A program of early childhood education must be predicated on three common goals: the maintenance of a learning atmosphere free of punishment, the emphasis on pupil self-discipline as a necessary survival skill, and the development of pupil respect for the acquisition and use of knowledge to ameliorate the colonized condition. Such a program is founded on two basic assumptions: that the individual learner, barring irreversible pre-natal or post-natal injury, has enough ability to meet the basic survival levels of school and society, and that language deficiencies resulting from undeveloped cultural communication patterns can broaden into deficiencies in reading skills, the single most important skill to academic achievement.

A program of early childhood education must begin with the home, the child's first learning environment. Here the child learns to perceive, to react to his perceptions, to formulate a value system from his many experiences, and to mesh these into a viable philosophical framework. As he grows older and more experienced, he is better able to recall experiences, to organize these into meaningful patterns, to reason in the abstract, to express relationships between his ideas and ideas from others, to combine his own ideas into new ideas, and to make judgments about the worth of his assessments. The parent has much to contribute to the success of the early childhood educational program. He may begin initially by communicating a positive attitude about the program to his children. This can be accomplished, behaviorally, by organizing the family home or apartment into three areas: a general area in which the total family might engage in group-related activities and discussions, a pupil study-activity area respected by the family members as the exclusive domain of the pupil, and a recreational-reinforcement area. The study activity need not be a private room. A corner of the living room, or a place under the stairwell can be converted into a satisfactory study area. A study table and chair, a lamp, and a dictionary are all that is needed to furnish the study-activity area.

A specific behavioral objective for the parent is to inculcate early in childhood the value of self-discipline. This may be accomplished with the parent supervising, but mostly, by encouraging the pupil to engage in activities for agreed upon periods of time in the pupil study-area. The activities may be direct school-related experiences such as spelling words, drawing pictures, and solving arithmetic problems. Activities indirectly related to school experiences may include putting together word puzzles, constructing model airplanes, and reading favorite comic books.

Participation in the recreational area where there is television and other pupil identified reinforcing activities might be made contingent upon the satisfactory participation in activities in the study area. The reinforcement area must not be used by parents as punishment mechanism. The parent must keep in mind the overall goal: to build in the pupil positive attitudes toward learning and the educational process. The child should not be required to spend more than 10 to 15 minutes daily in the study-activity area three or four evenings per week.

In the general area, activities may be planned around the discussion of common values held by the parent to be necessary to the survival of colonized people. It is imperative that discussions on the meaning of blackness begin in early childhood. The adolescent with a strong sense of ethnic-racial identity is less likely to succumb to false ideas and ideals about his racial heritage.

The daily early evening news telecast can be an excellent take-off point for family discussions. Hardly a day passes without the occurrence of some event having direct relevance to the survival of the colonized community. The alert parent will focus on these events, being careful to insure that the child is a full participant in the conversation. The family discussion is one way of developing the child's verbal fluency as well as social ease in expressing himself. The child should be taught that these are necessary survival skills for competing in a verbally oriented educational system and verbally oriented society.

The *Early Childhood Educational Center* is a transitional learning environment. It must be organized to combine the informality and accepting atmosphere of the home with some of the formal aspects of the school. The center should be within pupil walking distance of the home to minimize pupil and parent anxieties. The center might be sponsored by the local school board, a local church, or a group of community organizations. The sponsorship of a center can be a vehicle for facilitating community involvement in the education of colonized children. The center might be staffed with volunteer community people or paid professionals.

Selection of pupils may be made on the basis of maturity readiness, language readiness, or other criteria determined by the sponsoring community organization. A pupil's time in the center would vary with his needs.

The Early Childhood Center should be organized around three separate learning environments within each classroom: a task area, a pupil-reinforcement area, and a parent-pupil support area. Group and individually prescribed learning tasks would be carried out by the pupil in the task area, under the guidance of a *facilitator*. The term facilitator connotes subordination of the teaching process to the learning process, and a basic belief that the responsibility for learning should rest squarely on the shoulders of the learner. A parallel home task packet is provided each pupil. The scheduled home tasks are completed under the guidance of the parent. This is a direct way of involving parents in the educational development of their children. It is also a direct way of building parental accountability for the educational performance of their children. The parent-pupil support area provides a place for periodic parent-pupil support until the pupil can function independently of the parent. Together, the parent and the facilitator evaluate the readiness of the child for school.

All the educational activities at the Early Childhood Center should be designed to facilitate adjustment for the child into the receiver elementary school, the articulating middle and secondary schools and post-secondary schools, into the Adult Education-Marketable Skills Component.

The *Community Reinforcement Center* provides collateral supportive social-oriented activities that overlap those social activities carried out in the Early Childhood Center, the home, and the school. The Community Reinforcement Center is oriented to client drop-ins and stop-ins. The goal of the reinforcement center is to reinforce the ethnic/racial/cultural values of the clients. This is accomplished through ethnic literature, ethnic audio-visual materials, ethnic games, and other pupil determined activities. A phone-in tutor service based on a model developed by Dr. Samuel Sheppard for the St. Louis Banneker program might be available. Personnel staffing would include the use of audio-tutors. These are community resource volunteers or paid high school students who spend ten or fifteen minutes each day listening to a child read. The value is two-fold: it provides the child the opportunity to practice reading skills and at the same time reinforces his feelings of self-worth by having someone listen to him read each day.

A self-esteem tutor is the third member of the staff. Self-esteem tutors are community models with whom the client is able to identify in a growth motivation, yet non-threatening client-tutor relationship. The self-esteem tutor must have a strong personal relationship with his client since he will find it necessary, at times, to prod his client toward the accomplishment of a given objective.

Finally, the Community Reinforcement Center, in addition to being a learning environment for pupils, should be a vehicle for educational innovation and teacher-parent education.

The *Early Childhood Educational Model* presumes a central involvement role for the colonized parent. This is necessary for three-way accountability between pupil, parent, and educator. Further, the model presumes the presence in the home of parents or some guardians. This is essential if certain fundamental values are to be inculcated in early childhood. The model suggests the need for a national guaranteed income floor, an income adequate enough to make it possible for at least the mother, the heart of the family unit, to stay home.

The overriding goal of the early childhood educational program is to educate the child beyond the state of colonized mentality to a state of awakening. In this state of awakening he will exercise his affective and cognitive skills to recognize and deal with the human and structural colonizers that contribute to his oppression. From his state of awakening he can chart a deliberate course toward the goal of liberation.

The following excerpts were taken from a black student in a state of awakening that should prompt an awakening in educators:

In _____ city there are several alternative institutions which cater to the needs of some of those students who, for some reason or other, aren't going to the regular high school in their district. For some reason their regular high schools are too hard for them. It may be because they don't offer remedial reading and math classes for those who are just behind, or don't offer the additional help needed for them to compete in the average classroom situation.

For some students, it's the fact that, to them, the conventional high school as is, is hard for them to relate to and doesn't offer courses they feel are relevant to their individual needs. For others, who are not planning to continue their education, the high school courses that are required from most high schools just aren't needed.

There are some students who just need the type of environment such as _____ school just to catch up, or get themselves together enough so that they can go back to their regular school after having a baby, for example.

_____ school does not stress attendance. Rules aren't needed very often. The ones they do have aren't always enforced. In spite of all this, according to the counselor, there is no discipline problem. Each student is responsible for himself.

Some of the senior high school kids return in the afternoon to work as teacher aides, and are helpful in saying a few words to the younger kid who just acts up a little . . .

Everyone comes and goes without any hassle from the administration. Sure some of the students take advantage of this freedom, but it happens everywhere.

. . . In one history class I attended, I was especially impressed with the teacher. To me he was just unbelievably informed, and had a fantastic way of running his classes and presenting his material that really appealed to me.

. . . The class itself was held in a room that looked like a smaller version of what I thought our student lounge should look like, minus the ping-pong table, the coke machine. There were one or two couches, and a few chairs like the ones you sit in while your favorite dentist is keeping you waiting. I think I saw one straight back chair in that one room. The teacher did have a standard size desk, just like any other teacher, but I hardly noticed it, because he didn't use it to hide behind.

The teaching part of the class was held like a very informal group discussion, with the teachers presenting facts, and the students free to interrupt at any point in the discussion to ask questions, and to make points or comments. That day we started out talking about Papa Doc Duvalier, dictatorships, and Haitian economy. We talked about sugar in Cuba, the United States' interest and how much power the United States has in controlling the conditions of some smaller country's economies.

I was really impressed by the way he could tie so many things together, still making sense and maintaining a high level of interest in the class.

. . . The one thing I found that all teachers at _____ school had in common was that they were there because they wanted to be there. They didn't talk about the money or the physical surroundings, they talked about the students and the school itself . . . with sincerity.

The counselors have established what looks to me like an enviable relationship with the students. They can talk and they can relate.

I'm glad I had a chance to visit _____ school a second time. I got a better look, and I learned a valuable lesson. I don't think I'll look down upon another school because of the way they teach, or the students that go there . . .

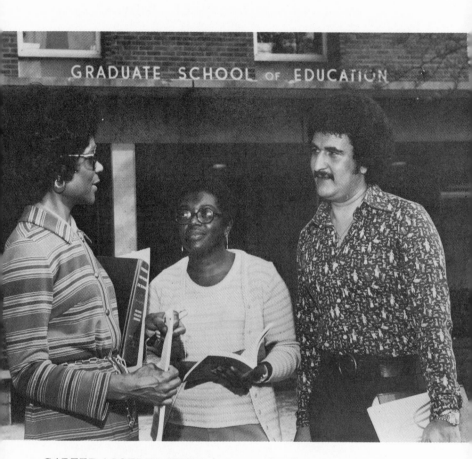

CAREER ACCELERATION. *In a special Career Opportunities Program at Rutgers Graduate School of Education, students are allowed to skip the bachelor's degree. Pictured opposite after receiving their master's degrees are, (l. to r.), Brooksie Cunningham, Beverly Wester and Charles Marrero.*

(all photographs by UPI Photo)

MODEL 4
Early Childhood Education For Colonized Children

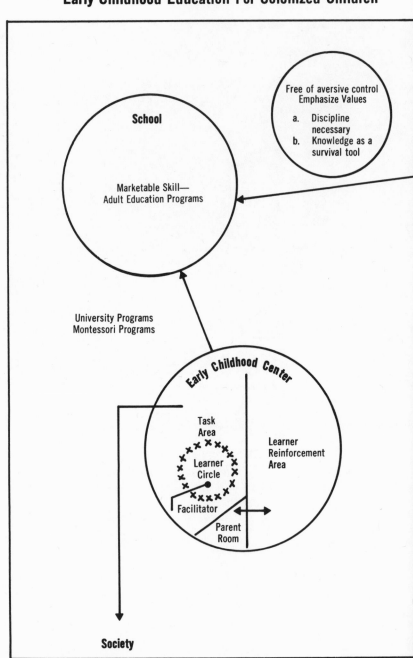

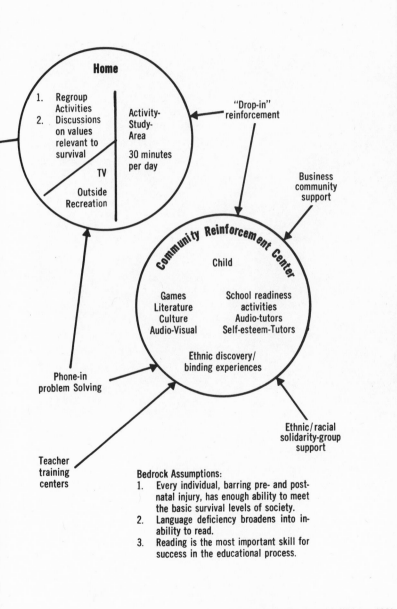

Home

1. Regroup Activities
2. Discussions on values relevant to survival

Activity-Study-Area

30 minutes per day

TV

Outside Recreation

"Drop-in" reinforcement

Business community support

Community Reinforcement Center

Child

Games
Literature
Culture
Audio-Visual

School readiness activities
Audio-tutors
Self-esteem-Tutors

Ethnic discovery/ binding experiences

Phone-in problem Solving

Teacher training centers

Ethnic/racial solidarity-group support

Bedrock Assumptions:
1. Every individual, barring pre- and post-natal injury, has enough ability to meet the basic survival levels of society.
2. Language deficiency broadens into inability to read.
3. Reading is the most important skill for success in the educational process.

WILSON C. RILES, the first black person to be elected to state-wide office in California, became Deputy Superintendent of Public Instruction for California in 1970. A liberal, Riles' primary concern is the welfare of school children.

DR. LEON SULLIVAN, *the first black director of General Motors, sponsors many black self-help programs, including the Advisory Council of Opportunities Industrialization Centers (OIC), an organization which trains black workers and finds jobs for them.*

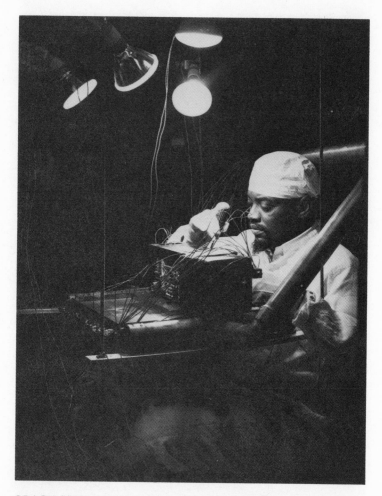

SPACE "SURGEON." At Honeywell's Radiation Center at
Lexington, Mass., technician Tom Peebles adjusts a navigation
instrument for a NASA satellite. The "operating room"
in this case is a chamber simulating space travel conditions.

PRODUCING PRINTED CIRCUITS FOR COMPUTER INDUSTRY. *Employee Andy Knox works on data processing equipment at Lockheed Electronics Company, Inc., preparing a board for silk screening.*

THOMAS BRADLEY, mayor-elect of Los Angeles, is the first black mayor of the nation's third largest city. Bradley, the son of a poor Texas fieldhand, is a city councilman who spent 21 years on the police force.

CHARLES EVERS qualified as the first black candidate for
governor in Mississippi. Photographed at a news conference
in front of the statue of the late Senator Theodore G. Bilbo
in the state capitol, Evers turned to the statue, saying,
"Your prediction (that blacks would be representing
Mississippi someday) has sure come true."

RONALD DELLUMS, U.S. Representative from California, and SHIRLEY CHISHOLM, U.S. Representative from New York, photographed at a press conference concerning George Washington University's OEOE, a federally funded urban law institute. Ms. Chisholm is the first black woman to be elected to Congress.

New York State Senator CONSTANCE BAKER MOTLEY, a
former lawyer for the National Association for the
Advancement of Colored People (NAACP), became the first
black woman federal judge. Mrs. Motley, seen here
chatting with Senator Jacob Javits, one of her sponsors,
was nominated as U.S. District Judge for the Southern
District of New York.

CHAPTER FIVE

The Colonized Parent

The United States Census Bureau this year disclosed
that the number of black families headed by women rose
in the 1960's—a clear indication to many authorities that
deepening poverty is causing social and family conditions
to deteriorate further in American ghettoes.
(James Steele, *The Progressive*, August, 1971, p. 24)

The black colonized parent has a challenge, a commitment,
and a charge. These must all be successfully met to insure the
delivery of educational services to colonized children. Every
parent seeks the best possible education for his child. Black
colonized parents in southern communities in particular have
made great personal sacrifices that their children could be
educated. Black mothers for generations have labored for as
little as $2.00 per week washing and ironing colonizer clothes,
cooking in colonizer kitchens, scrubbing colonizer floors, and
nursing colonizer babies—all so that their children could acquire an education. This unselfish love and staid commitment
to liberation for their children has provided the basis for the

development of an ethic peculiar to the ethos of the southern black colonized communities: a strong will and determination to succeed . . . in the educational system; in the economic system; and in the political system. This ethic has, without a doubt, been a sustaining force and a basis for communication and accountability between the black colonized pupil, the black educator, the black colonized parent, and the black community in general.

Black colonized parents have historically been strong supporters of community oriented schools. Expressions of such support have been manifest where a black student misbehaved in school, "sassed the teacher," or failed to follow through on a given assignment. In such instances, the word spread quickly through the black community, and in short order, mama was there standing in the classroom door with apron on, sleeves rolled up, and dish rag in hand to settle the problem. Papa paid his visit to the school only in four-alarm situations, since it was more difficult for him to leave his place of work. It is difficult to measure the effect that such expressions of support had on the achievement of black colonized children in spite of an educational environment that was at times openly hostile. I submit that the successes of black leaders and scholars can invariably be traced to certain manifest forms of parental support. But times have changed, and in today's black colonized community, as in the colonizer community, aversive control or discipline of students is frowned on as an effective way of motivating learners. A new set of values is emerging in the colonized community relating to the nature of education for colonized children, the relevance of education for colonized children, authority of educators, community involvement, and community control of schools. These emerging values will certainly be basic to the attitudes that will ultimately affect the behavior of colonized parents. This behavior may or may not be perceived by educators as being supportive of the school. Any support from the black colonized parent and community for the schools will be directly proportional to the commitment of educators to the education of their children.

The educational system, in the meantime, is likely to receive increasingly less support from the black colonized community as long as some forty-five percent of black men and women continue to leave public educational institutions without adequate marketable skills.

And so today, the black colonized community and the black colonized parent faces a challenge . . . a commitment . . . and a charge. The challenge is insuring the delivery of a relevant quality education to their children. A relevant quality education is seen by many parents as one which provides the colonized pupil with the skills to effectively deal with the conditions of colonization. Every parent must show his commitment by assuming full responsibility for the psychological and physiological development of his offspring . . . from pre-natal care to adulthood. Every black colonized parent has a charge, as a colonized parent, and as a member of the black community, to contribute to the collective aggrandizement of the colonized community.

Relevant education for colonized children must begin with the parent re-examining his own values regarding education, re-examining his own attitudes toward the educational system, re-examining its objectives as they relate to teaching and learning for black colonized children, and most importantly re-examining his behavior, in the presence of his children, in the presence of educators, and in the presence of the colonized community in general.

But let say a few words about relevant education! Relevant education can be a reality for black colonized children whose parents express positive attitudes and positive supportive behavior towards the school. Relevant education will be most difficult for colonized children to achieve when the values, attitudes and behavior of the parents are at cross-purposes with the school. Relevant education cannot be a reality for children whose parents see the school as a convenient depository, where, through some miracle, without their help, the pupil will be transformed into a self-sustaining citizen. It is true that a few exceptionally self-motivated students do achieve despite a lack of parental support. But, for the great majority of black colonized children, success will depend on parental persistence and most of all, parental push. That is the challenge . . . the commitment . . . and the charge.

Both the parent and the community must support the schools and public education in general. In the words of the late W. E. DuBois: "It is the public schools which can be, outside of the homes, the greatest means for training decent and self-respecting citizens."

The issues of racial-desegregation, integration, and racial separatism have become barriers to communication between many colonized parents and their children. These issues have indeed become a source of conflict in the colonized community in general. An Indian community in Minneapolis seeks Federal funding for an all-Indian school. The Chinese-Americans of San Francisco went to court in an effort to prevent their children from being transported to other areas of the city under city-wide court ordered desegregated plans. Increasing numbers of southern black communities are becoming disillusioned with school desegregation efforts. Many are demanding a return to all-black schools . . . all with the tongue in cheek "support" of racist white separatists.

But desegregation, integration, and separatism are only words. Relevance to black colonized people is the big question. Be alert—colonized community!

Black colonized parents and community in general must stand together on the premise that the relevance of integration to the community is relative to its condition of colonization. Simply stated, this means that integration/desegregation has very little relevance to the black colonized community when it is implemented under white colonizer rules. Integration under those rules has resulted in a disproportionate number of displaced black faculty members. Integration under those rules has meant the transportation of black children from their neighborhoods to often hostile white schools with bigoted teachers. Integration under colonizer rules has meant a general nonparticipation of black colonized pupils in the social activities of the school . . . no participation in the band . . . no participation in the speech club . . . no participation in the choir. (Participation in the athletic events is accepted on a purely pragmatic basis—coaching tenure is predicted on winning seasons. Such practices make it clear to the black colonized community that, in the eyes of the white colonizer, the heritage of the black community is not worth preserving or defending.) Integration under colonizer rules has meant the automatic closing down of schools in the black colonized community, no matter how recently the structure was built or how adequate the plant facility is. Too often all-black schools are closed down and made compensatory education centers. Compensatory education is needed in the colonized community, but to concentrate all the compensatory centers and vocational centers of the school system in the black community is to imply that colonized blacks are disinterested and unqualified to consider other educational areas. Further, the emphasis on the transportation of black children without equal emphasis on the transportation of white children implies a colonizer goal of destroying the black colonized community. Here the black parent and the black community in general must stand firm in the conviction that the colonized community is not to be destroyed. It is to be preserved . . . but without its prison-like conditions. This is the challenge . . . the commitment . . . and the charge.

Relevance of education to the black colonized community then is relative to the condition of colonization . . . and the black colonized parent must not succumb to blind faith in integration as a panacea for the educational achievement of their children. Quality relevant education can be achieved in a predominantly black school. A survey of schools by school achievement results in Los Angeles revealed a predominantly black school as the highest achieving school in the system. Further, an analysis of casual factors showed strong parental and community support for the school. And what about the fourth graders in an all-black rural Virginia school recording the highest reading score in the state? Let me make it clear again, I believe that quality relevant education can be achieved in a predominantly black school. Quality integrated education, however, cannot be achieved in either a predominantly white school or a predominantly black school. Further, the question of what is quality education and quality integrated education has never been defined at national, state or local levels.

Every black colonized parent must fulfill his individual commitment to the physiological needs of his child. The colonized parent must be cognizant of the statistics showing some 15 million hungry colonized people in this nation. He must be sensitive to what appears to be a deliberate effort to keep colonized people hungry. In this country, the grain and wheat farmers are being paid by our government under the Food Subsidy program to keep a certain number of acres out of production. Political and economic reasons matter little to me . . . all it says to me, behaviorally speaking, is that many black people are going hungry. And as educators we know that minds cannot properly function on empty stomachs.

The black colonized parent has a critical role to play in the psychological development of his children. The black colonized child has some values of his own, some of which are derived independently of parents. Many of these are at cross-purposes with parents. It is essential that the colonized parent's commitment include some understanding of today's youth.

One might raise the questions: what is commitment and who are the committed? In the black idiom, we say that a committed person is a person who is "together"—a person who is willing to do whatever is necessary to improve the black condition. These will most likely be people who dare to rock the boat. These are the human resources around which the black colonized community must rally. In the words of Frederick Douglas, "Those who profess to favor freedom yet deprecate agitation are men who want crops without plowing up the ground; they want rain without thunder and lightning; they want the oceans without the awful roar of its many waters."

The black colonized youth today are filled with a spirit of

liberation, and that spirit will not be suppressed or co-opted by the colonizer. That spirit of liberation also transcends considerations based on race.

The black colonized parent must commit himself to help black colonized youth to develop a rational mental perspective relating to the meaning of "blackness, the condition," "whiteness, the attitude," and all the racist manifestations of colonization. Many of today's black youth are desperately searching for ways to deal with the condition of Blackness. Many are committed to irrational ideas and racist-derived ideals, that, left unabated, result in negative end results for the individual, and collectively, for the colonized community. Parents must help youth to understand that what is needed in the colonized community is disciplined people who are willing to build a better black community. This is no easy task for hostile, jobless black youth as they daily assess their condition. It is a natural tendency to lash out in self-defense. Parents, therefore, must help their children to understand that there are productive ways of lashing out. You don't fight fire with fire; you fight fire with water. But fighting fire with water requires a disciplined mentality and parents must commit themselves to developing this quality in colonized youth. This is not an insurmountable task, as the great majority of today's youth are committed to the concepts of blackness, black pride, black people, and black power. Colonized parents must not be frightened by physical manifestation that affirm Blackness, such as the Afro hair style, the dashiki, the affinity for soulness. Instead, the black parent should use these as a focus to point out that the black community was developed on "soul," that the soul music enjoyed by today's youth is derived from the "blues" of yesterday, that the soul food that is today's delicacy was yesterday's staple, and that Frederick Douglas wore an Afro hair style and advocated black power and reconstructionism many years ago.

This does not mean that parents should not listen to youth. They must hear and listen to their children; parents must look and see what youth point to; they must keep abreast of the literature, language, and life style of their children. Parents must talk to and communicate with black youth. This can be accomplished, I submit, through a model educational alternative called *The Process to Intra-Group/Inter-Group Solidarity.* The process to black solidarity essentially encompasses four stages: the individual child, the black family, the school, and the larger community surrounding the school that is the black colonized community. The process is based on the assumption that the parents or guardians should be fully responsible for inculcating on the child those values necessary for survival. This model suggests a guaranteed annual income to every colonized family. Not a paltry sum, but one adequate enough to make it possible for the mother to stay at home with the children.

The black colonized child is the central focus of the process. The development of the child into a mature, "together" adult is the single purpose that connects the child, standing alone, making decisions affecting his own destiny; the child, as he relates to the family, the school, the black community, and other racial/ethnic solidarities of the colony.

In stage one, the colonized parent helps the child acquire a feeling of self-acceptance. This can be accomplished by having every child assume some responsibility for contributing to the everyday family experience. The child can be helped to understand that every family member must carry out certain responsibilities for the good of the family unit—that for him, school achievement is just as important as the parents' responsibility for providing food, clothing, and shelter.

The second stage should find the black colonized parent increasing the responsibility load on the child and raising his expectations for the child. There should be increasing activity designed to promote the independence of the child. Too many black children have become victimized by "momism," a phenomenon characterized by dominance of the mother image; this results in excessive dependence on the mother and ultimately in a lack of maturity and independence for the child. It is essential during this stage that the child be exposed to family discussions on the relevance of religion to blackness, of education to blackness, of the economic system to blackness, and the relevance of the political structure locally, state-wide, and nationally to blackness. The black child must be encouraged at this stage to utilize the resources of the total community, such as the city library, the recreational facilities, and all other public oriented social, religious, and educational programs offering opportunities for self-enlightenment. The black colonized parent's responsibility is to help the child to select from these offerings and relate them to his cultural heritage. Exposure to black models of humanity, particularly those from the black colonized community, can help the child to develop a strong base of racial/ethnic identity. Parents can contribute by providing opportunities for their children to see and talk to black electricians, black community organizers, black politicians, black foremen, black construction workers, black inmates, and black businessmen. The vision of the black child must not be limited to doctor, lawyer, teacher, or preacher—visions that are oftentimes unrealistic, frustrating and unachievable.

It is equally important that the sex role image be clarified early in childhood. The black colonized parent must erase any stereotypes about the housemaid role of the black female. Examples of women in science and technology should be pointed out from magazines, such as *Ebony* and *Jet*. The black single career woman and single career man should be discussed. A new role image for both sexes must be projected that will personify liberation and equality for both male and female. The black colonized parent must recognize that any acceptance of the concept of liberation must transcend the narrow limitations of either sex or race.

The self-image of the black child is central to his attitudes and behavior. Sociologists assert that self-image is the child's feeling about fate control—the feeling that one has control over his own destiny. The separatist contends that black colonized children achieve fate control best in all-black schools. This assertion is predicated on the belief that all-black schools are more likely to hold as a priority the development of the self-image of black colonized children. This position presumes further that black educators are central to developing positive self-images and positive feelings of fate control in black students. These are safe assertions. Proponents of integration, on the other hand, cite the studies showing that black children with positive fate control were found more often in integrated schools. I submit that studies such as these bring to surface the colonizer tactic of using colonized-derived data to affirm the rightness of whiteness.

A positive self-image developed in early childhood and nourished by parents will sustain the black child through many of the racial hostilities and dehumanizing conditions of colonization. Lillian Anthony, a noted black educator, once said that every black parent should provide his child a full-size ceiling to floor mirror, so that the child begins learning very early to appreciate the beauty that is his blackness.

The colonized parent must guard against making statements that suggest to the child he is anything less than a great human being. A common statement parents tend to make to their children is "make something of yourself." Obviously, that may be a well-intentioned statement, yet it has little relevance to youth. Parents must convey to black youth, by their attitudes and their actions, that the child is already something . . . something very special . . . and further, because he is something very special, both the parent and the community hold very high expectations for him. Another common-statement parents must avoid is: "You must prove yourself to Them." The message should be: "You don't have to prove anything to anybody, except yourself." Such positive expressions from the parent can do much to reinforce the child against the negative expressions he is sure to encounter as he moves from the family to the school setting.

In the third stage, the school setting, the black parent must intensify his efforts by working closely with teachers. The goal is enabling the child to compete successfully, socially and academically, in the total school experience. At this stage, there is a natural tendency for the black adolescent to seek transitory separatism . . . having lunch at an all-black table in the cafeteria, socializing in all-black cliques, and generally, exhibiting behavior proclaiming his commitment to Blackness. This should not be viewed with undue alarm by parents or educators. This behavior has always been manifest in all white student groups. Such practices should be accepted at face value for what they are—the exchanging of social amenities between children from common cultural backgrounds. Black parents and the black educator must not be alarmed because suddenly an all-black table in the cafeteria has higher visibility than the other all-white tables in the same room.

The primary concern of black colonized parents at the third stage of the process is the student's acquisition of cognitive and effective skills. Reading is the most critical skill area, and kindergarten to third grade is the critical time period for building this skill. The student who can read and handle numbers by the third grade has more than a 50 percent chance of completing his education. The student who is unable to read by the time he has completed the third grade is destined for academic failure and frustration. The parent and the community can play an important role in insuring that enough classroom emphasis is placed on reading. Colonized parents should insist that adequate time is spent each day in each classroom developing basic reading and computational skills. Parents must insist that there is accountability by individual student achievement, by classroom achievement, and by school achievement. If 32 children finish second-grade reading at or above grade level, the parents of all 32 pupils should be notified to provide sufficient summer reading experiences so that these skills are not lost over the vacation period. In the fall, the third-grade teacher should receive 32 pupils reading at or above grade level, and the cycle of accountability continues. This is three-way accountability between pupil, parent, and teacher. This cannot be accomplished, however, without the establishment of clearly stated reading behavioral objectives. The student, by the end of the sixth grade, should have acquired a state of basic literacy; he should be able to read from the daily newspaper with comprehension. He should be able to demonstrate competence in basic computational skills. He should be able to converse intelligently with others.

As the colonized black pupil moves into the forth stage, the black community, he becomes more community conscious, expressing the behavior and rhetoric of the moment in the community—the dress, the greeting, the taste for music, the choice of books to read and so forth. All of these are manifestations of black consciousness. It would be a mistake to generalize, saying that every black colonized adolescent behaves in a similar fashion. That is not the case. Because a black youngster does not go around greeting his brother with hand slaps and intricate handshakes, it does not mean that he is any less black-conscious or any less committed to ameliorating the conditions imposed by colonization. From this base of black consciousness the adolescent will develop awareness of the political, economic, and cultural dimensions of his existence. He will then begin his individual search for relevance and meaning. He will begin exploring his relationship to the total social structure.

The fifth stage of the process finds the black adolescent youth examining the relationship of the black colonized community to other racial/ethnic solidarities. He begins making economic and political comparisons of the relative power between groups; he begins to unravel many of the shibboleths surrounding equal opportunities, law and order, and due process. He recognizes the reality of the colony: power and redistribution of power, and from this base he begins a new day of commitment. Black colonized parents must encourage this awakening in their children, for awareness of social reality is a distinct characteristic of adolescence. While black children must become aware of the reality of the colony, they must not accept its continued existence as a reality. The black child must achieve a level of black consciousness that asserts:

> I am a Black American. Only I can define my freedom.
> No Preamble to a Constitution can make me free. No

Emancipation Proclamation can make me free. No
Declaration of Independence, Bill of Rights, Court Edict
or Constitutional Amendment can insure my freedom.
Freedom for me is a state of liberated mentality. There
are things within my control that I can, must, and will
do to bring about and sustain such a state of awakening.
I can develop my intellectual capabilities to a highly
productive level. I will condition myself to a high level of
political awareness. I will never be coerced or co-opted
against the goals of colonized people. I will be unyielding
in my conviction that a society to be truly humanized,
must first be decolonized. I will toil assiduously until
educational literacy, economic aggrandizement and
political power become realities . . . for colonized people
collectively. I will do all in my power to make this
world, a word in which all people . . . Black, Yellow, Red,
White and Brown can together share in equity, the
great, but yet-to-achieved potential for this planet:
Humanistic Justice, freedom from hunger and suffering,
peace and prosperity for all of that which is humanity.

Today's black colonized youth must be helped to understand
that black, as every other color, has a range of richness; that
soul is really without a color; that commitment to the struggle
for liberation is not the exclusive property of those under
thirty. Black colonized parents must help their children to
understand that there is little place in this struggle for the
undisciplined, the unskilled, and the unwilling to be skilled,
that there is little place in this struggle for those fol-
lowers who follow blindly the hard rhetoric of those who fail
to offer any specific, constructive alternatives to better life-
styles and life-chances for black colonized people, that there
is little place in this struggle for those self-appointed leaders
who qualify, not by their productive efforts or relevance to
the struggle, but by their obsequious postures to the colonizer.
Liberation of colonized children is the pervasive mission of
every black parent. It is his challenge . . . his commitment . . .
and his charge.

CHAPTER SIX

Education, Racism, and Human Behavior Change

This nation has failed to meet the challenge of individual and institutional racism in education. Efforts at school desegregation have been violently opposed, de facto segregation is prevalent in most urban school systems; public officials have openly defied court orders to desegregate schools. Federal legislation designed to aid schools attempting to desegregate continues to prohibit the use of funds for pupil transportation to achieve racial balance. Poor and minority children continue to be segregated in certain schools despite the multi-economic and multi-racial make-up of the entire community. Racism in America is escalating, states the report of the National Advisory Committee on Civil Disorders, and racial and/or economic isolation breed racism. Society, of itself, will not change, nor will wishing make it so. If the people of the colonized community wish to change the societal institutions of America, they must alter their own behavior patterns as well as those of the colonizer. Racism limits educational opportunities for colonized children, and the colonized community can ill afford any loss of human potential. Parents and teachers of colonized children must look to behaviorally oriented educational programs to counter the debilitating effects of individual and institutional racism.

Any discussion of programs designed to effect behavioral change must speak to the cognitive antecedents of behavior—values and attitudes. Behavioral changes derive from values and attitudes: values give rise to attitudes; attitudes precipitate behavior. Even though these terms, these phenomena of cognition, are abstract concepts, educators can manipulate them to eliminate racism. Values and attitudes are responsible for behavior that is racist or nonracist in nature. It is significant that these abstractions—behavior, attitude and value—can be isolated, programmed and taught.

We may infer an attitude from an observed behavior, and to the degree to which we modify an observed behavior, we can assume that we have altered an attitude. Behavioral changes can occur through compliance, through a subject's identification with a change agent or through internalization of a new set of values. Educators assume a significant responsibility as they exercise the prerogative of isolating certain values to be programmed into their pupils. Teachers, in effect, make value judgments of what one person presumes to be good for another person.

Programmed values are nothing new. Parents program values into their children. Advertising agencies attempt to program values into the entire population. Ministers, businessmen, politicians try to program people with a specific set of values and behavioral patterns to reflect those values. Schools, just as any other social institution, have the ability to affect as well as reflect certain values. In doing so, they have the potential to become a powerful counterforce to racist values generated in and transmitted through other social institutions.

Educators, in this context, should not only teach the pupil, but also teach the teacher a set of non-racist values. A general goal for educators should be to isolate specific teacher behavior observed by colonized pupils and their parents as being motivated by racism. The teacher should be presented with an alternative set of non-racist cognitive and behavioral skills. Observable behavior should then be assessed against a predetermined behavioral objective. It would then be possible to determine if the new behavioral skills had been internalized into a new set of values. Specifically, one approach might be to isolate and explode racist myths as a basis from which to establish a general goal: What behavior do we expect from a racism-free educator? What specific racist behavior do we as educators, pupils, and parents regard as reprehensible? Once general goals have been determined, we can proceed to define a specific behavioral objective.

Educational Alternative:
Racism in Education and Behavioral Change

Step One: Conduct a pre-assessment of the subject's knowledge about racism.

Step Two: Isolate and identify a racist myth.

Step Three: Explode the myth with factual data.

Step Four: Introduce a new alternative value.

Step Five: Introduce a new behavioral rule to reinforce this particular value.

Step Six: Provide the subject with a response-example showing him how he should have applied the behavioral rule.

Step Seven: Provide the subject with a question or set of circumstances in which he may try out his newly internalized behavioral rule.

Step Eight: Provide the subject with a response feedback so that he may know whether he applied the rule properly.

Step Nine: Provide the subject with a case study practice that he may try out his newly internalized rule.

A programmed behavioral approach may be developed along the same lines to help educators acquire skill in observing, recording, and reporting incidents of school conflict in behavioral terms. There are certain observable behavior similarities in incidents of conflict that can be described in terms of time, place, frequency, and duration of occurrence. These behaviorally described incidents can provide the administrator with a basis for better decision making through rational assessment as well as a tool for systematically observing, recording, and reporting incidents of conflict. Too often emotion and pressure prevent a good solution to school/community conflict. Teachers and administrators often fail to adequately cope with confrontations or student behavior problems because there are insufficient or conflicting descriptions of circumstances surrounding an incident. If teachers and administrators are to successfully resolve behavioral disturbances without further aggravating the tension between the students and the teachers or the school and the community, they must have a tool to facilitate a more accurate unbiased reporting of the observable details of incidents of conflict. Although individual perceptions of what happened will be based on and colored by the individual's own attitudes, values, and biases, a reporting instrument can be constructed that will elicit factual information regardless of perceptual distortions. A reporting instrument that provides a framework for the undistorted reconstruction of an incident of conflict will not only enable the administrator to intelligently and successfully resolve the conflict, but it also becomes an index from which to postulate inferences concerning attitudes and values from the observed behavior.

Educational Alternative:
A Constructural Framework for School Community Conflict

Behavioral Rule One: Know the environment and
dynamics of the community.

An educational cliché is that in order to teach a child well, you must know the child well. This truism must be extended to include his environment (the community) and life style. In order to intelligently resolve conflict, teachers and administrators need a working knowledge of the school/community—the geography, the economic, the political, and religious forces affecting the life style of the inhabitants of the colonized community. Housing patterns, territorial boundaries, socio-economic strata, and employment situation are all factors which affect conflict. This working knowledge must include a keen sensitivity to national, state, and local politics and policies affecting the community. To be responsive to the needs of a child, you must first determine what those needs are. The more a teacher knows about the life style of his pupils, the better he can determine needs and methods of ameliorating conflicting situations.

Behavior Rule Two: *Avoid using generalities when reporting negative incidents of behavior to parents and others.*

A major criticism from parents is the general nature of reports from the school on incidents of pupil misbehavior. Increasing numbers of colonized parents perceive these reports to be weighted with connotations of shame and failure, with subtle implications of parental, rather than school, failure. Unsubstantiated generalities are viewed by colonized parents as one more indication of institutional racism. An example of an unsubstantiated generality is the school principal who exercises a discretionary suspension, sending home the pupil with a note: "Suspended for being disrespectful and disruptive." The terms "disrespectful" and "disruptive" are generalities. When pressed, the principal attempts to justify his action with explanations such as, "He kicked in a glass door," or "Struck the hall aide in the face with a ruler." However, while these may be specific incidents, there is no mention of extenuating circumstances. Every report of an incident should be studied carefully before sending it to parents to be sure the specific negative behavior with surrounding circumstances is included. The increasing number

of confrontations between alienated pupils, parents, and
school personnel demands careful scrutiny by educators of
all outgoing verbal and written communications to the community.

Behavioral Rule Three: *Differences in perceptions, real or
imagined, are potential causes of
conflict, leading to behavioral consequences that must be dealt with.*

Seldom do two people see the same thing when observing
a given situation. Further, the idealist maintains that what we
see is not always real; the black soul idiom says, "Where it is
ain't necessarily where it's at." The old axiom that people tend
to see what they want to see and hear what they want to hear
has validity here. A school administrator fearing his efficiency
or authority threatened will tend to minimize the reporting of
incidents of conflict.

Administrators and teachers become targets of distorted
parent and pupil perceptions. The most important variable
affecting the image of the school is the perception of that
school in the eyes of the community. Alienated parents are beginning to perceive the ghetto as an institution invented by
the socio-political system bent on perpetuating colonization.
The school, as part of the system, shares the hostile feelings
of the colonized community. Two separate incidents come to
mind that illustrate behavioral consequences that sometimes
arise from real and imagined perceptions.

The first incident, which we shall call incident "A," was a
poster prepared by a social studies class that read "Keep the
White man in the White house." This poster appeared on the
classroom bulletin board as a part of a class project in which
the students were to come to class as presidential candidates
with a complete campaign presentation. The "white man in
the white house" poster was part of the presentation of the
student who came as a well-known southern white supremacy
politician. A black student not in the class observing the poster

came up with a perception based on his own attitudes and values. He reported that he saw a poster of a "black man hanging out of a garbage can under a caption 'Help keep America Clean'." The school principal, in trying to minimize the incident, had a different perception of the background of the incident. He stated that, "The students in that class knew what it was all about, but there are three classes that use that room and other students saw the poster as they passed in the hallway." In incident "B' the homeroom teachers were asked to approach talented black youths about the military service academies. Again, we have the matter of different perceptions. The principal and the school counselors perceived themselves as making a special effort to recruit black students for the military service academies. But to the black student, it was part of a campaign to route the black people off as cannon fodder and increase the already disproportionate percentage of black soldiers in Vietnam—a perception substantiated by ample statistics. These two separate incidents within the same school led to the following behavioral incidents of conflict. The words "kill the niggers" were chalked on a black student's locker and nobody could find out who did it; a 16 year old black student struck a teacher who failed him in Algebra and testified in juvenile court that he thought the teacher had called him a "nigger."

In observing incidents of conflict, the educator must be careful to document with behavioral specificity who did what to whom, where, and the frequency of occurence.

Behavioral Rule Four: Obtain a second witness prior to observing and recording incidents of conflict.

Since, in incidents of conflict, we cannot always be sure that our perceptions are accurate, we should, where possible, summon a second witness to observe an incident. The observers should focus on three role positions: 1) the *Target* (the receiving point at which the behavior is directed), 2) the *Objective* (the actor or source from which the target-directed behavior is emitted), and 3) the *Audience* (those witnessing but not participating in the conflict incident). There is behavioral objectivity in using the terms object, target, and audience. This is to avoid assigning labels such as "white boy," "Catholic girl," and other racist-oriented labels that may help to distort behavioral perceptual judgements.

Behavioral Rule Five: Call immediate conference with the involved parties and legal guardians, focusing on issues, not on personalities.

The educator of colonized children must not rely on the telephone and written notice as the sole means for parental notification for conference. He must use whatever resources are necessary, including taxi service and dispatching school personnel to contact parents at the home and place of work to insure their attendance at the conference. The educator must be prepared to take the conference to the parent in the event the parent is unable to come to the school. Social workers, nurses, home visitors, and even teacher aides can play a major role in home conferences. All should be instructed on behavioral methods of observing, recording, and reporting incidents of conflict before participation in home-school conferences on such incidents. It will be impossible for the school principal to mediate every conflict situation; however, since he must make the final disposition, his staff must provide him with all the appropriate behavioral data.

Specific sets of behavior are required of the person presiding at the conference, whether teacher, assistant principal, or principal. The participants in the conflict incident should be summoned to the principal's office to await the arrival of resource people, parents, and guardians. When all are assembled, the mediator introduces the students, the parents and the resource personnel. The mediator then begins the conference with a summary of the behavioral incident(s) and information provided by the staff. He should be careful to keep the focus on the summarized behavioral data, and not allow the discussion to shift to personalities. An attempt should be made to clarify the positions of the object, the target, and the teacher or school administrator. The object of the discussion is, of course, to reach a solution to the problem which caused the incident of conflict, and determine if further action is necessary on the part of the school (i.e., suspension) or one of the participants (i.e., restitution). If the issue is resolved to the mutual satisfaction of all parties involved, the signatures of the parties are collected on a special agreement/disagreement form (see p. 000). If the issue is not resolved, a second meeting should be scheduled. The mediator should then be prepared to make a decision, defer a decision where there is insufficient evidence, or refer the matter to a higher authority.

Models such as these presume that changing behavioral patterns of educators is possible through instruction reinforced with effective school system policies and procedures. Jean Grambs contends, "If persons can be educated to hate and distrust others, they can be educated to like and trust others." This is a basic premise of human relations programs. The models presented are a few of many possible alternatives to effective human relations education. It should be pointed out that these are only suggested alternatives to consider. In the final analysis, any effective human relations educational program must be developed to meet the needs of a particular school community.

The orientation and sensitizing of educators to the destructive power of racism cannot be left to chance, nor should it be relegated exclusively to human relations specialists. Human relations is everybody's job, from custodian to central staff, from secretary to superintendent, from bus driver to business manager.

There is nothing difficult about establishing an effective human relations program; it takes commitment, action, and resources. There may be difficulty in getting the commitment of many school boards, school administrators, and individual educators. It must be understood that without a clear statement of position from the school board delineating the educational goals of the school system in behavioral terms, a human relations program or a desegregation/integration program is defeated before it can begin. A statement, in detailed behavioral terms, of the objectives to be achieved, what is to be done, who is to do it, and how long it will take, must come from the school board as official district policy. The statement must also include the order of program priorities, and the allocation of financial and human resources reflecting commitment to the stated objectives.

Five major decisions must be made in designing a comprehensive human relations program: *First,* the school board/administration must decide on the goal to be achieved. Is it to share information? Is it to change behavior through the acquisition of new behavioral skills?

Second, it must be decided who will be the audience/recipients of the human relations instruction. Is the instruction to be directed to the faculty? To the students? Is it to be directed to parents and the community in general?

Third, there is the decision on the process, or how the goal will be reached. The school board must take a clear position as to whether change is being sought through identification, compliance, or the internalization of new values and the acquisition of new behavioral skills.

Fourth, a decision must be made about the methods and media for the program. Will case study materials be used? Will programmed materials be used? Will there be role playing and simulated game activities? Will there be confrontation-discussion activities? The question of the transferability of the programmed materials to real life situations can only be answered, in the absence of research, by experience. All one has to go on here is a basic contention of learning theorists that learning is facilitated when the learner can see the relationship between the theory he is learning, and the practical applicability of it.

Fifth, there is the decision of assessment. How will the school system determine whether the objectives set forth have been achieved? A strong endorsement is made here for behavioral assessment which presumes a detailed evaluation based on specific behavioral objectives. A case study programmed approach offers one such possibility; a study of cases can bridge the gap between theory and practice, and the use of case study materials should help the educator to gain a total perspective of a given situation through the exploration of components. The information gained from the assessment should help the school board and the administration to modify and ultimately improve the overall human relations program.

The elimination of racism from every level of the educational system—from classroom practices to school board policies—will require lasting attitudinal changes from both educators and pupils. This is a gargantuan task, calling for massive resources and national political commitment, neither of which has been forthcoming. Therefore, education must focus its efforts on an achievable goal—the behavioral change of administrators, teachers, and students. Poor black, poor Indian, poor white, poor Chicano children's opportunities must not be thwarted because of racism in education. Behavioral change must be the immediate goal; we cannot wait for additional change.

MODEL 5
Racism In Education And Behavioral Change
Programmed Education for Educators

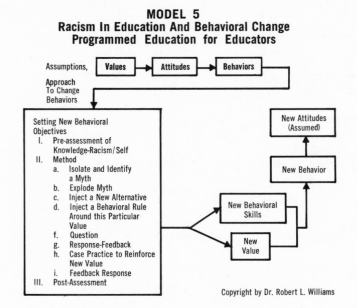

Copyright by Dr. Robert L. Williams

A CONSTRUCTURAL FRAMEWORK
FOR SCHOOL/COMMUNITY CONFLICT

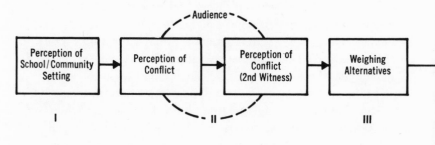

1. Climate
   - _____Temperature
   - _____Humidity
   - _____Date
   - _____Time

2. Friction-Conflict Domain
   - _____Classroom
   - _____Corridor
   - _____Girls Lavatory
   - _____Boys Lavatory
   - _____School Ground
   - _____Office
   - _____Gym
   - _____Cafeteria
   - _____Library
   - _____Bus
   - _____Shop

Who (object) _____
Did What _____
_____
_____
_____
_____
To Whom (target) _____
When _____
Where _____
Frequency of Occurrence _____

3. Actors Involved

Code		How Many										Example
____ A — Child: male		1	2	3	4	5	6	7	8	9	10	
____ B — Child: female		1	2	3	4	5	6	7	8	9	10	
____ C — Adolescent: male		1	2	3	4	5	6	7	8	9	10	
____ D — Adolescent: female		1	2	3	4	5	6	7	8	9	10	
____ E — Young Adult: female		1	2	3	4	5	6	7	8	9	10	
____ F — Young Adult: female		1	2	3	4	5	6	7	8	9	10	
____ G — Adult: male		1	2	3	4	5	6	7	8	9	10	
____ H — Adult: female		1	2	3	4	5	6	7	8	9	10	

B^1, D^1, D^5

Figure 1: The example shows an adolescent girl and a fifth adolescent girl direct-behaviors at a female child. B^1 is the target. D^1 and D^5 are the objects.

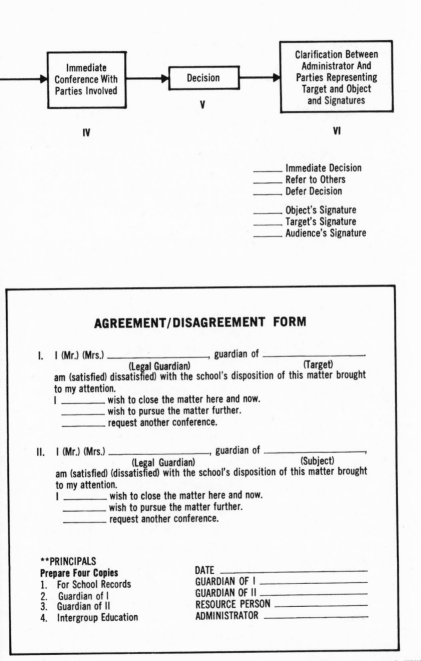

```
Immediate
Conference With    →    Decision    →
Parties Involved

IV                       V
```

Clarification Between
Administrator And
Parties Representing
Target and Object
and Signatures

VI

_____ Immediate Decision
_____ Refer to Others
_____ Defer Decision

_____ Object's Signature
_____ Target's Signature
_____ Audience's Signature

AGREEMENT/DISAGREEMENT FORM

I. I (Mr.) (Mrs.) _____, guardian of _____.
                  (Legal Guardian)   (Target)
    am (satisfied) dissatisfied) with the school's disposition of this matter brought
    to my attention.
    I _____ wish to close the matter here and now.
      _____ wish to pursue the matter further.
      _____ request another conference.

II. I (Mr.) (Mrs.) _____, guardian of _____,
                  (Legal Guardian)   (Subject)
    am (satisfied) (dissatisfied) with the school's disposition of this matter brought
    to my attention.
    I _____ wish to close the matter here and now.
      _____ wish to pursue the matter further.
      _____ request another conference.

**PRINCIPALS
Prepare Four Copies   DATE _____
1. For School Records   GUARDIAN OF I _____
2. Guardian of I   GUARDIAN OF II _____
3. Guardian of II   RESOURCE PERSON _____
4. Intergroup Education   ADMINISTRATOR _____

CHAPTER SEVEN

Aggrandizing the Colonized Community

We have studied and restudied the problems of the poor. Research and pilot programs for the "socio-economic strata," the "culturally deprived," and the "under-privileged," have provided adequate income for many . . . for new government bureaucracies, for research contract industries and other participants in the poverty industry. What people without money need most in order to live normal lives is money. (Senator Abraham Ribicoff, Reprinted by permission of *The New Republic*, © 1971, Harrison-Blaine of New Jersey, Inc.)

Job skills and employment are essential to the survival of the citizens of the colonized community. Much of the social unrest in the ghettoes of America can be attributed to conditions stemming from unemployment and under-employment. The colonized community, in order to achieve economic and political independence, must develop a strong base of economic power. Economic power is collectivized market power; it is the ability of the ghetto community to use its economic and political resources collectively to overcome conditions of colonization. An economic base of power can be only as strong, only as effective, as the quantity and quality of its gainfully employed human resources. The acquisition of job skills is of paramount importance to meeting a community's needs.

A strong base of economic power can be an effective instrument for positive political change. There is substantial evidence that dollars will increasingly dictate the direction and flow of politics. Aspiring black political candidates will be successful in proportion to their economic support. Richard Nixon is reported to have spent 12 million dollars in 1968 for broadcast advertising alone. The message to the colonized community is this—the tightening economic squeeze will force black candidates to seek greater economic sources of support. The colonized community must be ready and willing to provide such support.

Freeway construction which disrupts if not eliminates urban neighborhoods, and restrictive local housing codes will continue to be problems for colonized communities until such time as there are effective lobbies in Washington representing their interests. A strong economic base of power can be the supportive mechanism for such lobbies.

Quality education and equity of educational opportunity are abstractions that can be transformed through economic power bases into action program realities for colonized people. Gross educational inequities continue to exist between poverty stricken inner city schools and affluent suburban area schools. The widening gap can invariably be traced to economic disparities between city and suburban communities— disparities which provide the basis for many of the educational inequities in colonized schools. Such inequities are likely to be a reality for some time to come as long as the major share of public education is supported by local property tax revenues. Colonized communities with dwindling tax bases will find it increasingly difficult to keep pace with burgeoning affluent suburban communities. The same freeways that cut through inner city neighborhoods facilitate the exodus of people employed in the city to their homes in the suburbs where they spend and bank the money they have earned in the city. The inner city, already overburdened with a disproportionate share of socio-economic problems, will increasingly be called upon to provide greater services to the poor, the sick, the uneducated, the unemployed, the imprisoned, and the aged.

Colonized people have made personal contributions to the development of strong economic power bases in colonized communities. Some individuals have used economic gains from successful business ventures and investments to finance the educations of needy youth. But greater efforts must be made by a larger number of people to insure better opportunities for colonized children. Let us suppose that one hundred black sponsors each directed ten dollars a week to a guardian-in-trust fund in a black community bank for a pupil in first grade. At the rate of ten dollars a week, each child's trust account would grow to $520 plus the accrued interest per year; at the end of his senior year, each 18 year old would have $11,325. The net result is complete college or vocational financing for a colonized child and a strengthened community base of power from investments in black businesses.

Economic bases of power have historically been used as colonizer outer-city outposts to control inner city colonized people. This will continue to be the reality until there is some redistribution of economic power between colonizer and colonized and a greater number of economic power bases are developed in colonized communities. The ideals of power sharing and redistribution of power are contrary to the colonizer's creed of economic and political control. The ideal of economic aggrandizement must be a primary goal of colonized people. Strong economic power bases are not only essential to the growth of colonized communities, they are imperative for the good health of America's national social system. On the issue of power and colonizer-colonized relationships, two thoughts occur: the colonizer must learn how to share power; the colonized must learn how to use it.

Educational-Economic Alternative: The Development of Technical Skills for Economic Power Bases in the Black Colonized Community.

A program for developing technical skills can be implemented in two phases, the identification and training of unskilled human resources and the phasing of the newly skilled resources into industry. Phase one is implemented in nine steps:

Step One: A network of community resource persons is organized by a community sponsoring organization or a group of sponsoring organizations. Unskilled human resources are identified by members of the community resource network. The names of the unskilled are then referred to the sponsoring organization for follow-up.

Step Two: The sponsoring organization uses available information on job training programs, the job market, and the potential of the unskilled referrals as a basis for organizing information sharing seminars. These seminars should be conducted at sites where the resource potential is most accessible. These places are likely to be street corners and pool halls. Two objectives should be accomplished at each information sharing session: those in attendance should be informed of the available job opportunities, the job market, and employment skill requirements, and new recruits should be enrolled on the spot. The sponsoring organization must take great care to see that the information sharing sessions are staffed by knowledgeable resource persons. All printed materials to be disseminated should be carefully worded for clarity and easy reference.

Step Three: Each information sharing session should facilirate the identification and orientation of newly enrolled recruits.

Step Four: Each newly enrolled recruit referred to the sponsoring organization is assigned three network resource persons: a community person already gainfully employed, a vocational school counselor, and a third community person chosen by the recruit.

Step Five: Once in the program, the recruit is oriented to a broad range of career areas. The vocational school counselor underscores the necessity of developing economic bases of power in black colonized communities. The gainfully employed resource person emphasizes to the recruit some of the problems he is likely to encounter on the job. The recruit-chosen community resource person assures the recruit of his commitment to and support of the recruit through the initiation of his training to job placement. All three resource persons must impress upon the recruit the need for individual commitment to ameliorating the condition of colonization that imprisons the black community.

Step Six: After extensive guidance and counseling services with the three resource persons, the recruit makes his decision on the career training he will pursue.

Step Seven: Once a decision is made, the sponsoring organization insures enrollment of the recruit in a technical training program in the desired career field. Enrollment in the technical program is the culmination of a series of collaborative efforts between the recruit, the sponsoring community resource network staff, and the receiver-school training staff.

Step Eight: The recruit, now a trainee, will receive ongoing guidance and support from the sponsoring community resource network throughout his training period. The receiver-school counselor, working closely with the resource network staff, will arrange periodic on-site experiences for the trainee. Such experiences should include the observation of gainfully employed persons from the colonized community at work.

Step Nine: The trainee, upon completion of the training program, is referred by the training institution with the endorsement of the sponsoring community resource network staff, to an industrial organization for employment. The trainee, once gainfully employed, becomes a new member of the sponsoring community organization network. The resultant effect is two-fold: a yesterday's tax consumer becomes a self-supporting taxpayer, and the colonized community has gained another contributor to the economic base of power, thus strengthening the black community.

The establishment of a community organization resource network of skilled people has implications of national significance. Technical resources could be quickly mobilized and deployed to struggling colonized communities such as Fayetteville, Mississippi, and the ghettoes of urban cities. Contractors working on federally financed housing projects are required to actively recruit and hire minority group persons to meet eligibility requirements. An effective community organization resource network might be the mechanism to identify skilled colonized people nation-wide. Such skilled but unemployed persons could be deployed to projects seeking skilled minority-group persons. This would lay to rest once and for all the great colonizer dodge, "We would gladly hire skilled minority-group persons if only we could find them."

Educational-Economic Alternative: Phasing Black Americans into White Industrial Organizations.

The phasing of newly skilled black Americans into white industrial organizations can be successful where there is employer commitment to breaking the colonizing cycle of racism. Any program that accomplishes such an objective must rest on three assumptions: (1.) the economic system, more than any other system, holds the most potential for accomplishing social change; (2) a strong economic base of power in the black community is vital to the equilibrium of the national social system; and (3) black Americans, given the opportunities, can become self-determined productive citizens through gainful employment.

Three implementation steps are essential to phasing newly skilled blacks into white industrial organizations.

Step One: A decision of commitment to equal opportunity must be made by management. Communications training, sometimes called sensitivity training, is provided to management personnel to facilitate sensitivity to individual behavior as it influences others. Specifically, participants are expected to understand how communication is hindered because of overt and covert forms of racism. A general goal for communications training might be that of communicating more openly and effectively with others. Although there is insufficient evidence to show that attitudes are changed as a result of personnel participation in communications sensitivity training, such programs should still be worth considering if management is committed to the ideal that most human relationships can be improved.

Management personnel must be sensitized to the colonizing conditions of racism. This can be accomplished through a multiplicity of approaches, such as role-playing, confrontation group discussions, exposure to audio-visual materials, direct involvement in community sponsored projects, and regularly scheduled dialogue sessions with members of minority/colonized groups.

Management personnel must be cautioned against making racist assumptions about the unemployed blacks. The unemployment gap between whites and blacks gives credence to the contention that a significant number of potentially productive black Americans are jobless because of certain manifest forms of racism. Some 75 per cent of black Americans living in urban cities constitute a great reservoir of human potential, yet are assigned to the colonized heap. Management personnel must be sensitized against presuming that the black American entering a white industrial organization will be culturally empty handed. Nothing could be farther from the truth. The black worker will bring to the organization his newly acquired skills and the lifestyle that is reflective of his community background. Creative management must provide opportunities for these to be fully developed. Very little is known regarding the effects of the colonized community upon the aspirations and motivations of the black colonized worker. History, however, has shown that there has been a significant disparity between the aspirations of the black colonized worker and the opportunities afforded by management for achieving them.

Step Two: Management must insure the commitment of all personnel to the organization's goal—the successful phasing of black Americans into the organization. A clearly stated set of objectives leading to this goal should provide the basis for a series of management led workshops for all personnel. The workshops should be geared to helping the participants recognize and deal with various manifestations of racism. A general atmosphere of commitment should prevail in the organization. The pervasive organizational philosophy should be "equity of opportunity." There should be a concerted effort by management to dispel all notions that the newly arrived Blacks will be assigned exclusively to menial jobs. There should be direct instant promotions of Blacks demonstrating leadership potential. Here the organization's management will likely face charges of "preferential treatment" and "racism in reverse." But here is where management must take its stand. It must reaffirm its position that colonized people, to become full participating members of a social system that has systematically excluded them, will need preferential-compensatory assistance until the opportunity gap has been bridged successfully between the unfairly advantaged colonizer and the disproportionately oppressed colonized.

Step Three: A program for phasing black Americans into white organizations, to be successful, must be predicated on a clarification of role expectations between management and labor, and a base of follow-up support. It is essential that there be black professional specialists and black career counselors on staff. The presence of black models at all administrative levels should help to reduce the occasions when linguistic patterns and cultural behaviors become communications barriers between racial-ethnic groups.

The orientation program should place strong emphasis on continued individual guidance and support. Extensive supportive services such as health and safety rehabilitation programs should be provided. A strong supportive service program should include the establishment of day-care centers for working mothers. A guidance and extended aid system would facilitate the collective bargaining, developmental training, and compensation processes. Easy access to individual guidance and extended aid would characterize the *manpower utilization system*. It is also essential that there be two-way communications between the white supervisor and the black worker. There is need for well-defined communications processes.

Every system, every subsystem, every component, and every process should undergo continual evaluation. A systems analysis, in addition to evaluating production aspects of the organization, might be designed to alert management when non-discriminatory policies are not followed. Individuals and components contributing most to meeting the goal of phasing black Americans successfully into the organization should be rewarded. Efficient managers and production components are rewarded for good performance; the same principle might be applied to the elimination of behavioral manifestations of individual and institutional racism.

Educational-Economic Alternative: An Academy For the Study of relevant models to the Survival of the Black Colonized Community.

Any program designed to aggrandize the black colonized community must include a process and a procedure for disseminating and sharing information. It must provide the mechanism and the forum through which the black colonized community may periodically address itself to issues threatening its survival. A few of these are birth control, freeway displacement, and neighborhood abandonment, unemployment, metropolitanism, and economic manifestations of neo-slavery. These are issues to which the black colonized community must present a united community posture. A mechanism to facilitate the achievement of such a goal is the *mobile model-study academy*.

The academy is functionally a community action laboratory. It is a periodic gathering of black people to explore alternative models to better life styles and better life chances for the colonized community. The emphasis on model-study has special significance. Too often, black community groups make the mistake of attempting decision making in crisis situations. An incident of police brutality is the catalyst for a mass community meeting at which grievances are aired against the economic, educational, and political systems in general. Caucuses are called in an effort to expedite resolution of the grievances. But, too often, emotion and anger prevent group decision making; the evening will invariably degenerate into a rap session. A study of models will require community commitment to regular meeting dates. Alternatives and community positions must be agreed on before the crises; this will facilitate effective dealing with the crises. The study of alternative models will require a disciplined and sustained community effort.

An academy for the study of relevant models for the survival of the black community must be premised on three assumptions: (1) creative solutions to the survival of the black colonized community are latent in the minds of black people; (2) black enlightenment can be facilitated through a model study group interaction process; and (3), alternatives to survival must derive from new models reflecting the changing needs of the black community.

A community sponsoring steering committee for the academy solicits new models for presentation and study at the academy. Any person in the colonized community may offer new alternative models for study. Models are selected by two criteria: (1) the model must promise better political, educational, and social alternatives; and (2), the model is presumed by its author to be relevant to the present and/or future needs of the black colonized community. Every adult citizen in the colonized community is encouraged to be a regular and full participating member at academy sessions.

The format for each academy session is based on large group/small group/large group discussion. The call to order is followed by a presentation of the model selected for study. The presentation should be made by the author of the model. The presenter, using an overhead projector and overlays, details the objectives of the model, pointing out its strengths and weaknesses, and its promise of better alternatives. The presentation should take no more than 30 minutes. This will allow adequate time for large group and small group discussion before academy action is taken by roll call.

The small group discussions should provide every participant with full opportunity to express his concerns relative to the model under discussion. A moderator is assigned each small group with the responsibility of keeping group discussion directed to the model under study. A recorder is assigned to each small group to summarize the proceedings and make a report to the general membership. The large group is reconvened following the small group discussions at which time the recorder reports are heard. Academy action is taken on each model by a roll call to endorse the model, reject the model, or defer action on the model pending modifications. The official position taken by the academy is conveyed to the larger community as the posture of the black community speaking through the academy. This should silence the colonizer tactic of polarizing colonized communities and then raising the great question, "Who speaks for the black community?"

At the time of this writing, several critical issues face the colonized community. These, it would seem, should be the focus of academy discussion.

Birth Control. The United States Census Bureau reports that the black population of America has increased from 9.9 percent in 1920 to the present 11 percent. This does not appear to be substantial growth for black Americans over a fifty-two year period. The black community must explore the consequences of birth control. There are economic and political implications at the local, state, national, and international levels.

Freeway Displacement and Neighborhood Abandonment. Freeway construction in urban cities is displacing thousands of black colonized families at a time when housing for blacks is a critical problem. The problem is exacerbated as increasing numbers of state legislatures enact anti-low-income housing legislation. These measures will mitigate undue hardships on colonized blacks already overcrowded in ghettoes.

Clinics. Medical science appears to be on the brink of a process to replicate the human cell. This could lead to identical artificial replications of humanity. It has already been suggested by some that dancers and athletes should not be considered for replication. What should be the position of the black colonized community?

Alleged Economic Progress and Unemployment. Much has been said about the economic gains of colonized people. One recent report underscored the fact that in the north and west, black husband/wife families headed by persons under twenty-five years old earned a median salary equal to their white contemporaries. The report failed to note, however, that families in this category represented only three percent of all black families or that this percentage is in fact declining with the increasing unemployment among black men under twenty-five. The national unemployment rate for white Americans, at the time of this writing, is five percent. For black Americans, it is more than eight percent; for black youth, more than twenty-five percent.

Metropolitanism. There is a sudden interest in metropolitanism, the redistributing of political power bases to diffuse the voting power of colonized people. Three questions appear of critical significance. Should the long range political potential of concentrated colonized people be compromised in favor of short-range economic relief? Are black people willing to abandon the goal of racial separation for desegregation that would mean dispersal to suburban areas where their voting power will be diffused? Can the black colonized communities of large urban centers work together in a sustained effort to build effective economic and political power bases?

The academy can be a facilitating mechanism for productive problem solving seminars. It must never be allowed to become a mere congregation of colonized people where raps and resolutions are the agenda, caucuses and cocktails the modus operandi. The time is past for colonizer-directed conferences attempting to define for colonized people those issues only colonized people can define for themselves. The time is past for such conferences being convened in the glitter of uptown, away from the confines of colonized communities. These are not desirable practices to be emulated by colonized people since they are the practices of those who cause the oppression of colonized people.

There is a new economic and political awakening in the colonized community, but there is yet much to be done. California State Representative Ronald Dellums shares a few of his concerns:

> Our first order of business has to be to create a climate in this country that allows people to start re-evaluating whats being said to them, what's being fed to them in the newspapers, in the magazines, in political speeches.
>
> ... The Silent Majority is the most manipulated, programmed, duped group in this country ... they're overworked, underpaid, overtaxed and being exploited every single day.
>
> ... Talk about economic imperialism doesn't mean anything except to a cat who went to college. Break it down for the people so that they can understand that there's welfare for the rich in this country, that the real welfare programs are farm subsidies, oil depletion allowances, tax loopholes, cost plus war contracts.
>
> ... Black people are human beings in this country, and black people have a right to be for peace in Indochina just as any other human beings. Black people have a right to stand up and oppose the absurdity of sending our eighteen and nineteen year olds over there to be killed. Twenty-five percent of the deaths are black deaths; fifty-five percent of the casualties are black casualties. The reason is that they pass the tests low, so they end up on the front line. Can you understand that that has nothing to do with Vietnam? What it means is that racism in the educational institutions in this country shackles black soldiers and sends them to Vietnam to fight and die.
>
> ... It's the war that's at the basis of this economy man.

> How are we going to deal with the problems of
> education, housing, health care, guaranteed annual
> income, all the other issues that need to be addressed
> in this country so long as we spend fifty and sixty and
> seventy and 100 billion dollars a year for killing other
> human beings . . . most of them black or brown or poor
> people? (Ronald Dellums, *The Progressive*, June, 1971,
> pp. 17 & 18)

Sentiments such as these expressed by Congressman Dellums will be heard with increasing frequency from those concerned with the survival of colonized people. The social health of America is failing and Congressman Dellums has put the finger on the pain. Now the physician, the Conscience of America, must set into motion a diagnosis and a program of cure.

There is a new mood in the black colonized communities of America. Georgia State Representative Julian Bond has summoned black colonized people to a new South, and unity. And black Americans are heeding the call.

George Breathett, a noted educator, contends every black must return periodically to his "mecca," the South, for his self-renewal. To that we can only say "Amen." The return is not so much for the food, the fresh air, and the hospitality that is legendary, it is the warm fellowship that is the tie that binds the black communities and the black colonized people in the north, south, east, and west. But, to return is to have left. There is no leaving the South, for the South is more than a geographic entity, it is a part of the essence of what it is to be black in America.

Every black American, whether he is in Maine, Massachusetts, Mississippi, or Minnesota, must take his position for blackness and make his determined stand to prevail over the colonizing condition of oppression. A black man, as a red, yellow, brown or white man, must fulfill his ultimate destiny, the human imperative—Man the human being. The human imperative can be achieved only when there is change. There must be change, for the destinies of both colonizer and colonized are inextricably intertwined, and the common enemy destroying both is the pollution of racism. All vestiges of colonizer-colonized dichotomies must be resolved into a commonly shared humanity. And, insofar as ethnic, racial, economic, political, religious solidarities go, all are interdependent on the other. But the ultimate survival of this nation will depend on the positive contributions from all solidarities interacting as equal partners working for the common goal: a truly united United States of America.

MODEL 6
Development of Technical Skill for Economic Power Bases in the Black Colonized Community

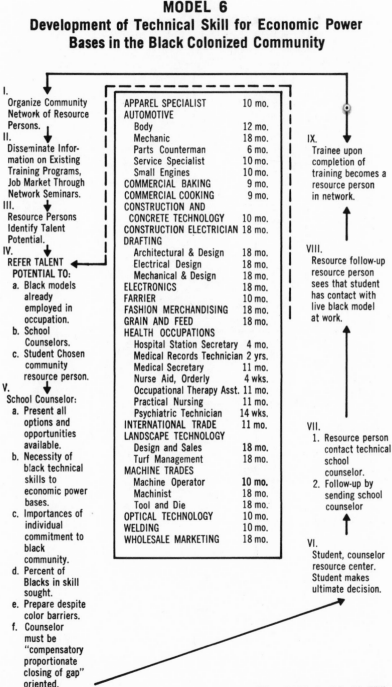

I.
Organize Community Network of Resource Persons.

II.
Disseminate Information on Existing Training Programs, Job Market Through Network Seminars.

III.
Resource Persons Identify Talent Potential.

IV.
REFER TALENT POTENTIAL TO:
a. Black models already employed in occupation.
b. School Counselors.
c. Student Chosen community resource person.

V.
School Counselor:
a. Present all options and opportunities available.
b. Necessity of black technical skills to economic power bases.
c. Importances of individual commitment to black community.
d. Percent of Blacks in skill sought.
e. Prepare despite color barriers.
f. Counselor must be "compensatory proportionate closing of gap" oriented.

APPAREL SPECIALIST	10 mo.
AUTOMOTIVE	
Body	12 mo.
Mechanic	18 mo.
Parts Counterman	6 mo.
Service Specialist	10 mo.
Small Engines	10 mo.
COMMERCIAL BAKING	9 mo.
COMMERCIAL COOKING	9 mo.
CONSTRUCTION AND CONCRETE TECHNOLOGY	10 mo.
CONSTRUCTION ELECTRICIAN	18 mo.
DRAFTING	
Architectural & Design	18 mo.
Electrical Design	18 mo.
Mechanical & Design	18 mo.
ELECTRONICS	18 mo.
FARRIER	10 mo.
FASHION MERCHANDISING	18 mo.
GRAIN AND FEED	18 mo.
HEALTH OCCUPATIONS	
Hospital Station Secretary	4 mo.
Medical Records Technician	2 yrs.
Medical Secretary	11 mo.
Nurse Aid, Orderly	4 wks.
Occupational Therapy Asst.	11 mo.
Practical Nursing	11 mo.
Psychiatric Technician	14 wks.
INTERNATIONAL TRADE	11 mo.
LANDSCAPE TECHNOLOGY	
Design and Sales	18 mo.
Turf Management	18 mo.
MACHINE TRADES	
Machine Operator	**10 mo.**
Machinist	18 mo.
Tool and Die	18 mo.
OPTICAL TECHNOLOGY	10 mo.
WELDING	10 mo.
WHOLESALE MARKETING	18 mo.

IX.
Trainee upon completion of training becomes a resource person in network.

VIII.
Resource follow-up resource person sees that student has contact with live black model at work.

VII.
1. Resource person contact technical school counselor.
2. Follow-up by sending school counselor

VI.
Student, counselor resource center. Student makes ultimate decision.

MODEL 7
Phasing Black Americans into White Industrial Organizations

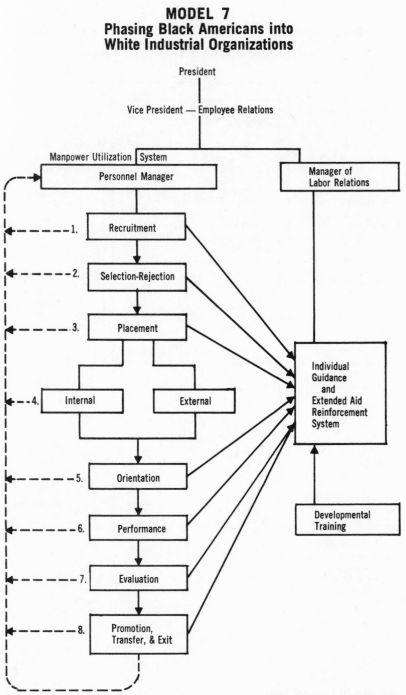

President

Vice President — Employee Relations

Manpower Utilization System

Personnel Manager

Manager of Labor Relations

1. Recruitment
2. Selection-Rejection
3. Placement
4. Internal   External
5. Orientation
6. Performance
7. Evaluation
8. Promotion, Transfer, & Exit

Individual Guidance and Extended Aid Reinforcement System

Developmental Training

MODEL 8
An Academy for the Study of Relevant Models to the Survival of the Black Colonized Community

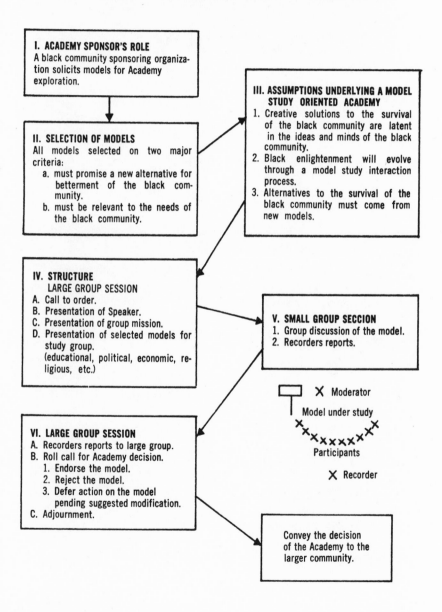

I. ACADEMY SPONSOR'S ROLE
A black community sponsoring organization solicits models for Academy exploration.

II. SELECTION OF MODELS
All models selected on two major criteria:
  a. must promise a new alternative for betterment of the black community.
  b. must be relevant to the needs of the black community.

III. ASSUMPTIONS UNDERLYING A MODEL STUDY ORIENTED ACADEMY
1. Creative solutions to the survival of the black community are latent in the ideas and minds of the black community.
2. Black enlightenment will evolve through a model study interaction process.
3. Alternatives to the survival of the black community must come from new models.

IV. STRUCTURE
LARGE GROUP SESSION
A. Call to order.
B. Presentation of Speaker.
C. Presentation of group mission.
D. Presentation of selected models for study group. (educational, political, economic, religious, etc.)

V. SMALL GROUP SECCION
1. Group discussion of the model.
2. Recorders reports.

X Moderator
Model under study
Participants
X Recorder

VI. LARGE GROUP SESSION
A. Recorders reports to large group.
B. Roll call for Academy decision.
  1. Endorse the model.
  2. Reject the model.
  3. Defer action on the model pending suggested modification.
C. Adjournment.

Convey the decision of the Academy to the larger community.

Bibliography

A. BOOKS

Allport, Gordon. *The Nature of Prejudice.* Garden City: Doubleday, 1958.

Ardrey, Robert. *Territorial Imperative and African Genesis.* New York: Atheneum Press, 1966.

Argris, Chris. "T-Groups for Organizational Effectiveness." *Creative Personnel Management.* Boston: Allyn Bacon, 1966.

Baldwin, James. *The Fire Next Time.* New York: Dell, 1968, p. 40.

Bennis, Warren G. "Changing Organizations." *The Journal of Applied Behavioral Science.* II:3 (July-August-September, 1960), pp. 247-263.

Bloom, G. F., and H. P. Northrup. *Economics of Labor Relations.* Homewood: Irwin, 1965.

Carmichael, S. and C. Hamilton. *Black Power: The Politics of Liberation in America.* New York: Vintage Press, 1967.

Clark, K. *Dark Ghetto.* New York: Harper & Row, Publishers, 1965.

Cleaver, Eldridge. *Soul on Ice.* New York: Dell, 1970.

Daily, Charles A. "Elimination of Operating Prejudice."

Research Annual on Intergroup Relations. New York: Frederick A. Praeger, 1966.

Dalton, M. *Men Who Manage.* New York: John Wiley and Sons, Inc., 1959.

Davis, A. and J. Dollard. *Children of Bondage.* Washington: American Council on Education, 1940.

Eddy, E. *Walk the White Line.* New York: Anchor Books, 1967, Chapter VII.

Everett, Downing and Leavitt. *Case Studies in School Supervision.* New York: Holt, Rinehart and Winston, 1962.

Fanon, Frantz. *The Wretched of the Earth.* New York: Grove, 1968.

Foltz, D. *The World of Teaching Machines.* Washington: Electronic Teaching Laboratory, 1967.

French, Wendell. *The Personnel Management Process.* Boston: Houghton Mifflin, 1964.

Gage, N. *Handbook of Research on Teaching.* Chicago: Rand McNally and Co., 1963.

Ginzberg, Eli. *The Development of Human Resources.* New York: McGraw Hill, 1966.

Gross, N. *Who Runs Our Schools?* New York: John Wiley and Sons, Inc., 1958.

Halpin, A. *Theory and Research in Administration.* New York: MacMillan, 1966.

Hemphill, J. *Dimensions of Administrative Performance.* New York: Teachers College, Columbia University, 1961.

Herriot, R. and N. Hoyt. *Social Class and the Urban Schools.* New York: John Wiley and Sons, Inc., 1966.

Himes, Joseph S. "Some Work-Related Cultural Deprivations of Lower Class Negroes." *Poverty in America.* Ann Arbor: The University of Michigan, 1965.

Hueber, Donald E. "Human Relations and Industry." *Research Annual on Intergroup Relations*. New York: Frederick A. Praeger, 1966.

Kozol, J. *Death at an Early Age: The Destruction of the Hearts and Minds of Negro Children in the Boston Public Schools*. Boston: Allyn and Bacon, 1947.

Labor Policy and Practice "Personnel Management Section." Bureau of National Affairs. IV:20, June 29, 1961.

Lazarfeld, P. and W. Theilens. *The Academic Mind*. Glencoe: The Free Press, 1958.

Lerner, M. "City Lights and Shadows," *America as a Civilization*. New York Simon and Shuster, Inc., 1957.

March, J. and H. Simon, *Organizations*. New York: John Wiley and Sons, Inc., 1958.

McKersie, R. and R. Walton, *Behavioral Theory of Labor Negotiations*. New York: McGraw-Hill, 1965.

New World Dictionary of the American Language (College Edition). New York: World Publishing Co., 1968, p. 288.

Parsons, Talcott. *Sociological Theory and Modern Society*. New York: Free Press, 1967.

Quarles, Benjamin. *Frederick Douglas: Great Lives Observed*. Prentice-Hall, Inc., 1968, p. 49.

Raskin, Marcus. *Reconstruction or Revolution*.

Roget's International Thesaurus. New York. Thomas Y. Crowell & Co., 1964.

Report of the National Advisory Commission on Civil Disorders. New York: The New York Times., 1968.

Rummler, Geary R. "Programmed Learning—A Progress Report." *Creative* Personal Management. Boston: Allyn & Bacon, 1967.

Sargent, C. and E. Belisle. *Educational Administration: Cases Concepts.* Boston: Houghton-Mifflin Co., 1955.

Seiler, J. A. *Systems Analysis in Organization Behavior.* Homewood: Dorsey, 1967.

Simmel, G. and K. Wolff. *The Sociology of George Simmel.* Glencoe: The Free Press, 1950.

Stagner, R. and H. Rosen. *Psychology of Union-Management Relations.* Belmont: Wadsworth Publishing Co., 1965.

Stember, C. *Education and Attitude Change.* New York: Institute of Human Relations Press, 1961.

Stouffer, S. *Communism, Conformity, and Civil Liberties.* New York: Doubleday, 1955.

Strom, R. *Teaching in the Slum School.* Columbus: Charles E. Merrill Books, Inc., 1965.

Tannenbaum, Arnold S. *Social Psychology of the Work Organization.* Belmont: Wadsworth Publishing Co., 1966.

United States Department of Education, Health and Welfare. Title Four under the Civil Rights Act.

United States Department of Labor. *Occupational Outlook Handbook.* Washington: U.S. Government Printing Office, 1966-67.

Weber, M. *The Theory of Social and Economic Organization.* New York: Oxford University Press, 1947.

Wortman, Max. ed. *Creative Personnel Management.* Boston: Allyn & Bacon, 1966.

Yolder, Dale. *Personnel Management and Industrial Relations.* Englewood Cliffs: Prentice-Hall, 1956.

B. PERIODICALS

Becker, J. and B. Geer. "The Fate of Idealism in Medical School," *American Sociological Review, XXXIII,* February, 1958, pp. 50-56.

Bidwell, C. "Some Effects of Administrative Behaviors: A Study of Role Theory," *Administrative Science Quarterly.* 1957-58, pp. 481-500.

Chase, F. "Professional Leadership and Teacher Morale," *Administrator's Notebook,* Vol. 1, No. 8, March, 1953.

Cornell, F. "Socially Perceptive Administration," *Phi Delta Kappa,* Vol. 37, March 1956, pp. 219-223.

Davison, H. and G. Lang. "Children's Perceptions of Their Teachers' Feeling Toward Them Related to Self-Perception, School Achievement, and Behavior." *Journal of Experimental Education,* XIX, 1969.

Dearborn, D. and H. Simon. "Selective Perception: A note on the Departmental Identifications of Executives," *Sociometry,* 1958, pp. 140-144.

Dunkel, H. "Value Decisions and the Public Schools," *The School Review.* Chicago: University of Chicago Press, 1962, pp. 163-170.

Emans, R. *Journal of Educational Research,* VII, March, 1966, p. 59.

Flanagan, J. "The Critical Incident Technique," *Psychological Bulletin,* July, 1954, pp. 327-358.

Gage, N. "Paradigms for Research on Teaching," *Handbook of Research on Teaching.* Chicago: Rand McNally & Co., 1963, p. 95.

Getzel, J. and E. Guba. "Social Behavior and the Administrative Process," The School Review, Winter, 1957, pp. 423-441.

_____, Adminstration as a Social Process," Administrative Theory in Education. Chicago: University of Chicago Press, 1958.

Gouldner, A. "Cosmopolitans and Locals: Toward an Analysis

of Latent Social Roles," *Administrative Science Quarterly*, 1957-58, pp. 281-444.

Grambs, J. "Methods and Materials in Intergroup Education," *Poverty Education and Race Relations: Studies and Proposals*. Boston: Allyn and Bacon, 1947, p. 140.

Greenberg, Paul. "St. Richard in the School Bus Dragon." *Minneapolis Star*, August 12, 1971, p. 6D.

Groff, P. "Dissatisfactions in Teaching the Culturally Disadvantaged Child," *Phi Delta Kappa*, XXXXV, February, 1963, p. 75.

Grusky, O. "Corporate Size Bureaucratization and Managerial Succession," *The American Journal of Sociology*, LXVII (November), 1961, pp. 261-269.

Hamilton, C. "Education, Race and New Political Arrangements," *NEA Journal*, February, 14-16, 1968.

Heider, F. "Attitudes and Cognitive Organization," *Journal of Psychology*, May, 1946, pp. 107-112.

Henry, J. "The Formal Structure of a Psychiatric Hospital," *Psychiatry*, XVII, May, 1954.

Holland, J. "Research on Programming Variables," *Teaching Machines and Programmed Learning II Data and Directions*. New York.

Knoll, Erwin. "Representative Ron Dellums: Black, Radical and Hopeful." *The Progressive*, June, 1971, pp. 17 & 18.

Mack, R. "The Changing Ethnic Fabric of the Metropolis," *The Schools and the Urban Crises*. Chicago: Holt, Rinehart and Winston, 1966, p. 41.

Maccoby, H. "Controversy, Neutrality, and Higher Education," *American Sociological Review*, XXV, 1960, pp. 884-893.

Maslow, A. "A Theory of Human Motivation," *Psychology Review*, 1943, pp. 370-396.

Smith, B. "Patterns of American Prejudice," *Anti-defamation League Bulletin*, XXV, April, 1968.

Spindler, G. "Education in Transforming American Culture," *Harvard Educational Review*, XXV, February, 1955, pp. 145-156.

Steel, Ronald. "The World We're In: An Interview with Walter Lippman," *New Republic*, November 13, 1971, p. 22.

Steele, James B. "The Abandoned Cities," *The Progressive*, August, 1971, p. 24.

Stone, J. "The Effects of Learner Characteristics on Performance in Programmed Text and Conventional Texts Formats," *Journal of Educational Research*, LIX, 1965, pp. 122-127.

Thompson, J. "Organizational Management of Conflict," *Administrative Science Quarterly*, March 4, 1960.

C. UNPUBLISHED MATERIALS

Amos, R. "Comparative Accuracy with Which Negro and White Children Can Predict Teacher Attitudes Toward Negro Students," Unpublished Ph.D. Dissertation, University of Michigan, 1951.

Dreikurs, R. "The Courage To Be Imperfect," A Position Paper, 1942.

Parsons, T. "On the Theory of Influence," A Position Paper, 1962.

Spanjer, A. "Processes of Interpersonal Influence," A Position Paper, 1967.

Minneapolis Tribune, May 18, 1968, p. 1.

Minneapolis Tribune, September 17, 1968, p. 1.

Name Index

Subject Index